CHOOSING VICTORY OVERCOMING DEFEAT

KAY ARTHUR

D0051302

HARVEST HOUSE PUBLISHERS
Eugene, Oregon 97402

Except where otherwise indicated, all Scripture quotations in this book are taken from the New American Standard Bible, © 1960, 1962, 1963, 1968, 1971, 1972, 1973, 1975, 1977 by The Lockman Foundation. Used by permission.

Except where otherwise indicated, all maps and charts in this book, as well as the *"How to Use the Inductive Study Approach"* portion of the introductory material, have been adapted and condensed from the *International Inductive Study Bible*, Copyright © 1992, 1993 by Precept Ministries.

Cover by Left Coast Design, Portland, Oregon
Cover illustration and interior art by Micha'el Washer

The International Inductive Study Series
CHOOSING VICTORY,
OVERCOMING DEFEAT

Copyright © 1995 by Precept Ministries
Published by Harvest House Publishers
Eugene, Oregon 97402

Library of Congress Cataloging-in-Publication Data

Arthur, Kay, 1933–
    Choosing victory, overcoming defeat : Joshua, Judges, and Ruth /
Kay Arthur.
        p. cm. — (International inductive study series)
        ISBN 1-56507-304-5
        1. Bible. O.T. Joshua—Study and teaching. 2. Bible. O.T. Judges—Study
and teaching. 3. Bible. O.T. Ruth—Study and teaching. I. Title.
    II. Series: Arthur, Kay, 1933–   International inductive study series.
    BS1295.5.A78   1995   95-6977
    227'.2'007—dc20   CIP

All rights reserved. No portion of this book may be reproduced in any form without the written permission of the Publisher.

Printed in the United States of America.

98 99 00 01 02 03 / BP / 13 12 11 10 9 8 7 6 5 4 3

CONTENTS

How to Get Started . . .

Reading directions is sometimes difficult and hardly ever enjoyable! Most often you just want to get started. Only if all else fails will you read the instructions. I understand, but please don't approach this study that way. These brief instructions are a vital part of getting started on the right foot! These few pages will help you immensely.

FIRST

As you study Joshua, Judges, and Ruth, you will need four things in addition to this book:

1. A Bible that you are willing to mark in. The marking is essential. An ideal Bible for this purpose is *The International Inductive Study Bible (IISB)*. The *IISB* is in a single-column text format with larger, easy-to-read type, which is ideal for marking. The margins around the text are wide for note-taking.

The *IISB* also has instructions for studying each book of the Bible, but it does not contain any commentary on the text, nor is it compiled from any theological stance. Its purpose is to teach you how to discern truth for yourself through the inductive method of study. (The various charts and maps that you will find in this study guide are taken from the *IISB*.)

Whatever Bible you use, just know you will need to

mark in it, which brings me to the second item you will need . . .

2. A fine-point, four-color ballpoint pen or various colored fine-point pens that you can use to write in your Bible.

3. Colored pencils or an eight-color Pentel pencil (available at most office supply stores).

4. A composition book or notebook for working on your assignments and recording your insights.

SECOND

1. As you study Joshua, Judges, and Ruth, you will be given specific instructions for each day's study.

Remember, anytime you get into the Word of God, you enter into more intensive warfare with the enemy. Why? Every piece of the Christian's armor is related to the Word of God. And our one and only offensive weapon is the sword of the Spirit, which is the Word of God. The enemy wants you to have a dull sword. Don't cooperate! You don't have to!

2. As you read each chapter, train yourself to ask the "5 W's and an H": who, what, when, where, why, and how. Asking questions like these helps you see exactly what the Word of God is saying. When you interrogate the text with the 5 W's and an H, ask questions like this:

    a. **What** is the chapter about?

    b. **Who** are the main characters?

    c. **When** does this event or teaching take place?

    d. **Where** does this happen?

    e. **Why** is this being done or said?

    f. **How** did it happen?

3. The "when" of events or teachings is very important and should be marked in an easily recognizable way in your Bible. I do this by putting a clock like this: ⏰ in the margin of my Bible beside the verse where the time phrase occurs. You may want to draw the clock over the time-related word or phrase, or you may want to underline or color the references to time in a specific color.

Remember, time may be expressed in several different ways: by mentioning an actual year, month, day, or by mentioning an event such as a feast, a year of a person's reign, etc. Time can also be indicated by words such as *then, when, afterwards, at this time,* etc.

4. You will be given certain key words throughout the books of Joshua, Judges, and Ruth. Marking key words is the purpose of the colored pencils and the colored pen. If you develop the habit of marking your Bible in this way, you will find it will make a significant difference in the effectiveness of your study and in how much you remember.

A **key word** is an important word that is used by the author repeatedly in order to convey his message to his reader. Certain key words will show up throughout the book; others will be concentrated in specific chapters or segments of the book. When you mark a key word, you should also mark the key word's synonyms (words that mean the same thing in the context) or pronouns *(he, his, she, her, it, we, they, us, our, you, them, their)* in the same way. I will give you suggestions for ways to mark key words in your daily assignments.

Marking words for easy identification can be done by colors or symbols or a combination of colors and symbols. However, colors are easier to distinguish than symbols. If I use symbols, I keep them very simple. For example, I color *repent* yellow but put a red diagram like this over it **repent**. The symbol conveys the meaning of the word—a change of mind. When marking key words, do it in a way that is easy for you to remember.

When I mark the members of the Godhead (which I do not always mark), I color each word yellow. But I use a purple pen and mark the Father with a triangle like this **God**, symbolizing the Trinity. I mark the Son this way **Jesus**, and the Holy Spirit like this: **Spirit**.

You should devise a color-coding system for marking key words throughout your Bible so that when you look at the pages of your Bible, you can see instantly where specific key words are used.

When you start marking key words, it is easy to forget how you are marking them. I recommend cutting a three-by-five card lengthwise and writing the key words on that. Color-code the words and then use the card as a bookmark. You may want to make one bookmark for words you are marking throughout your Bible, and a different one for any specific book of the Bible you are studying.

When you are instructed to mark a key word, the word is the *New American Standard* translation of the word. However, if the *King James Version* (KJV), the *New Kings James Version* (NKJV), or the *New International Version* (NIV) translates the word differently, the word used in those translations is given to you in a footnote.

5. Because locations are important in a historical or biographical book of the Bible, you will also find it helpful to mark these in a distinguishable way. I simply

Therefore, ask God to reveal His truth to you, to lead you, and guide you into all truth. He will, if you will ask.

THIRD

This study is designed to put you into the Word of God on a *daily* basis. Since man does not live by bread alone but by every word that comes out of the mouth of God, we each need a daily helping.

The assignments for each week cover seven days; however, the seventh day is different from the other days. On the seventh day, the focus is on a major truth covered in that week's study.

You will find a verse or two to memorize and STORE IN YOUR HEART. Then there is a passage to READ AND DISCUSS. This will be extremely profitable for those who are using this material in a class setting. It will cause the class to focus their attention on a critical portion of Scripture. To aid the individual and the class, there's a set of *Optional Questions for Discussion*. This is followed with a *Thought for the Week* which will help you understand how to walk in the light of what you learned.

When you discuss the week's lesson, be sure to support your answers and insights from the Bible itself. Then you will be handling the Word of God in a way that will find His approval. Always examine your insights by carefully observing the text to see *what it says*. Then, before you decide *what a Scripture or passage means*, make sure you interpret it in the light of its context.

Scripture will never contradict Scripture. If it ever seems to, you can be certain that somewhere something is being taken out of context. If you come to a passage that

underline every reference to location in green (grass and trees are green!) using my four-colored ballpoint pen. Maps have been included in this study so you can look up locations in order to put yourself into context geographically.

6. When you finish studying a chapter, record the main theme of that chapter on the AT A GLANCE chart under the appropriate chapter number. The chart is provided for you at the end of each book in this study. (If you have an *IISB*, you will want to record the chapter themes on the AT A GLANCE chart at the end of each book in your Bible (then you will have a permanent record of your studies right at your fingertips).

7. If you are doing this study within the framework of a class and you find the lessons too heavy, simply do what you can. To do a little is better than to do nothing. Don't be an "all or nothing" person when it comes to Bible study.

8. Always begin your studies with prayer. As you do your part to handle the Word of God accurately, you must remember that the Bible is a divinely inspired book. The words you are reading are truth—given to you by God that you might know Him and His ways.

> For to us God revealed them through the Spirit; for the Spirit searches all things, even the depths of God. For who among men knows the thoughts of a man except the spirit of the man, which is in him? Even so the thoughts of God no one knows except the Spirit of God (1 Corinthians 2:10,11).

symbols. However, colors are easier to distinguish than symbols. If I use symbols, I keep them very simple. For example, I color *repent* yellow but put a red diagram like this over it **repent**. The symbol conveys the meaning of the word—a change of mind. When marking key words, do it in a way that is easy for you to remember.

When I mark the members of the Godhead (which I do not always mark), I color each word yellow. But I use a purple pen and mark the Father with a triangle like this **God**, symbolizing the Trinity. I mark the Son this way **Jesus**, and the Holy Spirit like this: **Spirit**.

You should devise a color-coding system for marking key words throughout your Bible so that when you look at the pages of your Bible, you can see instantly where specific key words are used.

When you start marking key words, it is easy to forget how you are marking them. I recommend cutting a three-by-five card lengthwise and writing the key words on that. Color-code the words and then use the card as a bookmark. You may want to make one bookmark for words you are marking throughout your Bible, and a different one for any specific book of the Bible you are studying.

When you are instructed to mark a key word, the word is the *New American Standard* translation of the word. However, if the *King James Version* (KJV), the *New Kings James Version* (NKJV), or the *New International Version* (NIV) translates the word differently, the word used in those translations is given to you in a footnote.

5. Because locations are important in a historical or biographical book of the Bible, you will also find it helpful to mark these in a distinguishable way. I simply

3. The "when" of events or teachings is very important and should be marked in an easily recognizable way in your Bible. I do this by putting a clock like this: ⊛ in the margin of my Bible beside the verse where the time phrase occurs. You may want to draw the clock over the time-related word or phrase, or you may want to underline or color the references to time in a specific color.

Remember, time may be expressed in several different ways: by mentioning an actual year, month, day, or by mentioning an event such as a feast, a year of a person's reign, etc. Time can also be indicated by words such as *then, when, afterwards, at this time,* etc.

4. You will be given certain key words throughout the books of Joshua, Judges, and Ruth. Marking key words is the purpose of the colored pencils and the colored pen. If you develop the habit of marking your Bible in this way, you will find it will make a significant difference in the effectiveness of your study and in how much you remember.

A **key word** is an important word that is used by the author repeatedly in order to convey his message to his reader. Certain key words will show up throughout the book; others will be concentrated in specific chapters or segments of the book. When you mark a key word, you should also mark the key word's synonyms (words that mean the same thing in the context) or pronouns *(he, his, she, her, it, we, they, us, our, you, them, their)* in the same way. I will give you suggestions for ways to mark key words in your daily assignments.

Marking words for easy identification can be done by colors or symbols or a combination of colors and mark in it, which brings me to the second item you will need . . .

2. A fine-point, four-color ballpoint pen or various colored fine-point pens that you can use to write in your Bible.

3. Colored pencils or an eight-color Pentel pencil (available at most office supply stores).

4. A composition book or notebook for working on your assignments and recording your insights.

SECOND

1. As you study Joshua, Judges, and Ruth, you will be given specific instructions for each day's study.

Remember, anytime you get into the Word of God, you enter into more intensive warfare with the enemy. Why? Every piece of the Christian's armor is related to the Word of God. And our one and only offensive weapon is the sword of the Spirit, which is the Word of God. The enemy wants you to have a dull sword. Don't cooperate! You don't have to!

2. As you read each chapter, train yourself to ask the "5 W's and an H": who, what, when, where, why, and how. Asking questions like these helps you see exactly what the Word of God is saying. When you interrogate the text with the 5 W's and an H, ask questions like this:

    a. **What** is the chapter about?

    b. **Who** are the main characters?

    c. **When** does this event or teaching take place?

    d. **Where** does this happen?

    e. **Why** is this being done or said?

    f. **How** did it happen?

How to Get Started . . .

Reading directions is sometimes difficult and hardly ever enjoyable! Most often you just want to get started. Only if all else fails will you read the instructions. I understand, but please don't approach this study that way. These brief instructions are a vital part of getting started on the right foot! These few pages will help you immensely.

FIRST

As you study Joshua, Judges, and Ruth, you will need four things in addition to this book:

1. A Bible that you are willing to mark in. The marking is essential. An ideal Bible for this purpose is *The International Inductive Study Bible (IISB)*. The *IISB* is in a single-column text format with larger, easy-to-read type, which is ideal for marking. The margins around the text are wide for note-taking.

The *IISB* also has instructions for studying each book of the Bible, but it does not contain any commentary on the text, nor is it compiled from any theological stance. Its purpose is to teach you how to discern truth for yourself through the inductive method of study. (The various charts and maps that you will find in this study guide are taken from the *IISB*.)

Whatever Bible you use, just know you will need to

CONTENTS

Except where otherwise indicated, all Scripture quotations in this book are taken from the New American Standard Bible, © 1960, 1962, 1963, 1968, 1971, 1972, 1973, 1975, 1977 by The Lockman Foundation. Used by permission.

Except where otherwise indicated, all maps and charts in this book, as well as the *"How to Use the Inductive Study Approach"* portion of the introductory material, have been adapted and condensed from the *International Inductive Study Bible*, Copyright © 1992, 1993 by Precept Ministries.

Cover by Left Coast Design, Portland, Oregon
Cover illustration and interior art by Micha'el Washer

The International Inductive Study Series
CHOOSING VICTORY,
OVERCOMING DEFEAT

Copyright © 1995 by Precept Ministries
Published by Harvest House Publishers
Eugene, Oregon 97402

Library of Congress Cataloging-in-Publication Data

Arthur, Kay, 1933–
    Choosing victory, overcoming defeat : Joshua, Judges, and Ruth /
Kay Arthur.
        p. cm. — (International inductive study series)
    ISBN 1-56507-304-5
    1. Bible. O.T. Joshua—Study and teaching. 2. Bible. O.T. Judges—Study
and teaching. 3. Bible. O.T. Ruth—Study and teaching. I. Title.
II. Series: Arthur, Kay, 1933–   International inductive study series.
BS1295.5.A78 1995   95-6977
227'.2'007—dc20   CIP

All rights reserved. No portion of this book may be reproduced in any form without the written permission of the Publisher.

Printed in the United States of America.

98 99 00 01 02 03 / BP / 13 12 11 10 9 8 7 6 5 4 3

CHOOSING VICTORY OVER- COMING DEFEAT

KAY ARTHUR

D0051302

HARVEST HOUSE PUBLISHERS
Eugene, Oregon 97402

is difficult to deal with, reserve your interpretations for a time when you can study the passage in greater depth.

Books in *The International Inductive Study Series* are survey courses. If you want to do a more in-depth study of a particular book of the Bible, we suggest you do a Precept Upon Precept Bible Study Course on that book. You may obtain more information on these studies by contacting Precept Ministries, P.O. Box 182218, Chattanooga, TN 37422, 423/892-6814, or by filling out and mailing the response card in this book.

JOSHUA, JUDGES, AND RUTH

How absolutely awesome it is, my friend, to know that you and I can actually choose victory. The children of the world, who are by nature sons of disobedience, do not have that option—unless of course they repent and believe on the Lord Jesus Christ.

But because we are the children of God, victory is always ours for the obedience of faith. And that is what Joshua, Judges, and Ruth is all about—choosing victory and not defeat by hearing and obeying the Word of God. Victory is faith's guarantee. No matter what comes your way, no matter what you face, you can be more than a conqueror through Him who loves you!

Choosing Victory, Overcoming Defeat is a study that will take you back to the Old Testament which was "written for our instruction, that through perseverance and the encouragement of the Scriptures we might have hope" (Romans 15:4). And hope you will have, if you will give yourself to this study and do it as unto the Lord!

As you interact with the Word of God day in and day out over these next weeks, you are going to find yourself face to face with history—and with the God of history. It has been said that history is "His Story." How true! It is the account of God's dealing with and ordering the affairs of man. However, it is also the account of what happens when man chooses to believe and obey God and what happens when he doesn't. How does God respond in the face of man's disobedience? Is there a way for man to turn around? And what if he doesn't? Does it only affect him? Can the disobedience of one man affect a family, a society, a nation?

As you study, gathering the holy manna by which man is sustained, you will find the answers to these questions and more. And you will discover for yourself how to choose victory rather than defeat!

JOSHUA

Week One

How Can You Be Strong and Courageous?

Day One

As you know from reading "How to Get Started," it is helpful to make a bookmark for any book of the Bible you are studying so that you can write down and remember all the key words you plan to mark in that book.

Remember that not all key words appear throughout the entire book. Some are specific to a particular chapter or section. In the book of Joshua, you will mark some words throughout the book, but with each section of the book you will add some words to your bookmark that are specific to that section. You will be given the key words for each section as you work so you can add them to your bookmark!

The book of Joshua can be divided into four sections: chapters 1–5, 6–12, 13–21, and 22–24. The first section can be called "Preparing to Enter the Land." As we begin our study on this book, list the following key words on your bookmark and begin to mark them as they appear: *God, LORD, Joshua, land,*[1] *strong,*[2] *courageous,*[3] *firm, command*[4] *(commanded*[5]*), covenant, possess*[6] *(possession*[7]*), ark of the LORD (ark of the covenant), and Israel.*[8] Remember to mark any pronouns or synonyms that refer to each of these words. Don't forget to underline in a special color every geographical reference. If you can't locate a city or region, it is because the exact location is unknown. As you come to any location references, look them up on the map on page 22.

Watch for what you can learn about the Lord as you work through the book too! Noting how the Lord is described and what you learn about Him throughout the book of Joshua and as you study other books of the Bible will teach you much about your God! If you begin a list on what you learn about Him, be sure to leave adequate room to allow you to add to it throughout your study. To know Him is to love and trust Him. Daniel 11:32b says that the people who know their God will be strong and do exploits (KJV).

Now read Joshua 1 and mark any of the key words listed on your bookmark. As you read, carefully observe who is speaking, to whom they are speaking, and what is being said. Always interrogate the text with the 5 W's and an H: who, what, when, where, why, and how. Asking these questions will give you much insight, and you will find that you can handle the Word of God with greater integrity because those questions make you stay close to what the text of Scripture says and helps keep you from interpreting the text incorrectly.

When you finish reading and marking Joshua 1, list in your notebook God's commands and promises to Joshua. You should leave several pages open so that you can add what you learn about Joshua as you continue to study! Record the theme of this first chapter on the JOSHUA AT A GLANCE chart (page 48).

DAY TWO

It will be profitable for you to stop at this point and do a little background reading on Joshua. You will come to appreciate how Joshua came to the position he has in Joshua 1.

Read Exodus 17:8-13; 24:12,13; 32:17. (Note that Joshua was not in the camp with the people who sinned; he was at the mountain waiting for Moses to come down.) Read Numbers 13:1-16,25–14:10,26-38; Deuteronomy 32:44; 34:1-12. Watch for every reference to Joshua, and mark these if you like. You may want to note these verses from Exodus, Numbers, and Deuteronomy which shed more light on Joshua as cross-references in the margin of your Bible beside Joshua 1:1. Cross-referencing helps when you can't remember the location of a passage that sheds light on or correlates with the one you are studying. Cross-referencing is also very helpful when you do not have your study notes with you because your notes are right in your Bible! So, to help you later, write these cross-references in the margin of your Bible close to the appropriate text in Joshua.

Add to the list on Joshua you began yesterday in your notebook the basic facts you learn about him from these cross-references. Think about the kind of man that God chose to replace Moses. Could God have chosen you?

DAY THREE

Read Joshua 2. Once again mark any of the key words

you see. However, since Rahab becomes a major character in this chapter, also mark in a special way every reference to *Rahab* and any pronouns that refer to her. Also
mark the word *heard* in this chapter and then observe
what was heard, by whom, and the effect it brought. (You
don't need to add either reference to your bookmark.)

In your notebook, list all you learn from this chapter
about Rahab and also add to your list on Joshua.

Record the theme of chapter 2 on your JOSHUA AT
A GLANCE chart (page 48).

DAY FOUR

Read Joshua 3 and 4. Again mark the key words. Be
sure you mark geographical locations in this chapter.
Remember, all of these events take place around the
Jordan River. When you go to the map on page 22 to
locate these areas, find the Jordan River on your map and
go from there.

Carefully observe what God does in these chapters
and why He does it. Marking every reference to *Joshua*
(and any pronouns referring to him) and listing what you
learn in your notebook will help you see what God does!

Be sure not to miss how the Lord is described in this
chapter! Add any insights to the list you began. If you
haven't started it, be sure to begin one today.

If you have room in the margin of your Bible, next to
Joshua 4:19, you might want to write the date and what
happens on that date. There's a Jewish calendar on page 23.
Note the Babylonian name for the first month and write it,
along with the day, in the margin of your Bible next to 4:19.

List in your notebook any new insights on Joshua that you glean from these chapters. Also record the theme of Joshua 3 and 4 on the JOSHUA AT A GLANCE chart (page 48).

DAY FIVE

Read Joshua 5 and mark any key words listed on your bookmark. Also mark the word *circumcised*[9] *(circumcise, circumcising*[10]*)*. I mark it this way circumcised. (Sometimes it helps to know how someone else marks a word since there are just so many colors and symbols you can use, so I share them to be helpful!)

It would be good to note in the margin of your Bible what happens in verses 10, 11, and 12 of chapter 5. Also mark when these things take place.

Give special attention to Joshua 5:13-15.

DAY SIX

Today you will begin a new section in Joshua. This second section can be called "The Conquest of the Land" and encompasses Joshua 6–12. Continue to mark the same key words, if they appear, that you marked in the first section, but now add these key words to your bookmark: *fear*,[11] *fight*[12] *(fought*[13]*)*, and *captured*.[14] Mark key words as they appear in the text, and remember to mark any pronouns or synonyms which refer to these words.

*Joshua:
Occupying
the Promised
Land*

Mediterranean
(Great) Sea

Sidon
Mt. Lebanon
Damascus
Mt. Hermon

Ahlab
Tyre
Beth-shemesh
Dan (Laish)
Kedesh

Achzib
Hazor
Merom
BASHAN
Acco
Beth-anath?
Rehob
Aphek
Sea
of
Galilee
(Chinnereth)
Golan
Ashtaroth

SIDON
ASHER
NAPHTALI
ZEBULUN
Shimron
Mt. Tabor
Kishon
River
ISSACHAR
Dor
Megiddo
Jezreel
Taanach
Ibleam
Beth-shan
Yarmuk River
Edrei
Ramoth-gilead
Jabesh-gilead
GILEAD
ARAM

MANASSEH
Hepher
Tirzah
Jordan River

Mt. Ebal
Mt. Gerizim
Shechem
Succoth
Jabbok River
GAD
AMMON
Joppa
Aphek
Shiloh
EPHRAIM
Bethel
Jazer
Rabbah
Shaalbim
Ai
Jericho
Gezer
Gibeon
Gilgal
Ekron
Aijalon
BENJAMIN
Shittim
Heshbon
Ashdod
DAN
Jerusalem
Bezer
Libnah
Kiriath-jearim
Mt. Nebo
(Pisgah)
Ashkelon
Gath
Adullam
Beth-shemesh
REUBEN
Beth-zur
Gaza
Eglon?
Lachish
Hebron
Gerar
Debir
Dead
Sea
Aroer
Ziklag?
JUDAH
Arnon River
Beer-sheba
Arad
MOAB
Hormah
Kir-hareseth
SIMEON
Wilderness of Judah
Zoar
Tamar
Zered Brook
EDOM
NEGEV
Kadesh-barnea
?–Approximate location

The Jewish Calendar

Babylonian names (B) for the months are still used today for the Jewish calendar. Canaanite names (C) were used prior to the Babylonian captivity in 586 B.C. Four are mentioned in the Old Testament. **Adar-Sheni** is an intercalary month used every two to three years or seven times in 19 years.

1st month	2nd month	3rd month	4th month
Nisan (B) Abib (C) March-April	Iyyar (B) Ziv (C) April-May	Sivan (B) May-June	Tammuz (B) June-July
7th month	*8th month*	*9th month*	*10th month*
5th month	**6th month**	**7th month**	**8th month**
Ab (B) July-August	Elul (B) August-September	Tishri (B) Ethanim (C) September-October	Marcheshvan (B) Bul (C) October-November
11th month	*12th month*	*1st month*	*2nd month*
9th month	**10th month**	**11th month**	**12th month**
Chislev (B) November-December	Tebeth (B) December-January	Shebat (B) January-February	Adar (B) February-March
3rd month	*4th month*	*5th month*	*6th month*

Sacred calendar appears in black • Civil calendar appears in gray

Read Joshua 6. When you mark the key words, also look for the phrase *under the ban*[15] and mark it in a distinctive way. (I just underline it several times in black.) You'll also want to mark every reference to *Rahab* as well as any pronouns or synonyms which refer to her. Mark these as you did in Joshua 2.

In this chapter observe where the ark of the covenant (ark of the Lord) is placed in the Israelites' lineup as they march around Jericho. Watch and mark time phrases in a distinctive way. You may want to put a clock like this: 🕐 over the phrase and/or in the margin.

When you finish marking every reference to Rahab and observing what you learn from the text about her, read Matthew 1:5[16] and rejoice in the awesome grace of God.

Note the curse that is put on anyone who would try
to rebuild Jericho. Although there is a modern city called
Jericho, the ancient city was never rebuilt.

Make sure you have recorded the themes of chapters
5 and 6 on the JOSHUA AT A GLANCE chart (page
48).

Don't forget to add any new insights on Joshua and
Rahab to your lists.

DAY SEVEN

📖 Store in your heart: Joshua 1:7,8 (or 1:7-9).
Read and discuss: Joshua 1:1-9; 2:8-14; 6:6-16.

OPTIONAL QUESTIONS FOR DISCUSSION

❧ What are God's commandments and promises for
Joshua and the people?

 a. What is Joshua told to do in respect to the Word
 of God?

 b. What do you think it means to be "strong and
 courageous"?

 c. What did you learn about Joshua from your study
 this week? What about Joshua caused God to put
 him in the position of being a leader of Israel? Was
 he a proven or unproven man?

 d. At this point, what do you learn about Joshua that
 you can apply to your own life?

∾ How does God validate Joshua's leadership before the people? In what way does this action show that as God was with Moses, He was also with Joshua?

∾ What are the children of Israel told to do before they crossed over the Jordan and before they go against Jericho?

∾ What events take place at Gilgal? What is the significance of these events?

∾ What do you learn from Rahab about the reputation of the Israelites?

    a. How do you think this attitude affected the inhabitants of Jericho when they saw the Israelites marching around Jericho?

    b. What kind of a reputation does Rahab have? Yet, what does God do with Rahab and why?

∾ What do you think the children of Israel learned about God from the battle of Jericho? What did you learn about God from Joshua 1–6?

THOUGHT FOR THE WEEK

When God says something, He stands by His Word to perform it. The promises of God are "yea and amen" (2 Corinthians 1:20). In Genesis 15, God told Abram (Abraham) that his descendants, the Israelites, would be strangers in Egypt, enslaved and oppressed for 400 years. He further told him that in the fourth generation they would return to the land God had promised to him and his descendants forever. However, because the iniquity of the Amorites (the people who lived in Canaan) was not yet complete (Genesis 15:1-16), this promise would not be fulfilled for 400 years! Now the 400 years were complete, and God was about to fulfill His Word.

You and I can always trust God! What God says will come to pass, but only in His time and in His way. Your responsibility is to know His Word! You are not to simply hear it and then "let it depart out of your mouth." Rather, you are to meditate on it day and night, and do all that He commands you. What God commands, at times, may not be the way you would accomplish something. After all, who would attack a city by marching around it six times, expecting the walls to come down after the seventh time around by blowing trumpets and shouting?

Your place is not to question God, nor doubt Him—but to obey Him. When you obey the Word of God, no matter how things look or seem, you are being strong and courageous.

You become strong and courageous when you meditate on God's Word. Knowing the Word will help you to not turn to the right or to the left. Instead, you will walk in God's straight and narrow path, and then you will have success and prosper in God's way. We will possess what God has ordained for us. Who could want anything more!

Are You Going for Something "Under the Ban"? Watch Out!

DAY ONE

In order to refresh your memory about God's instructions to Israel when they conquered Jericho read Joshua 6 again. Then read Joshua 7. As you read Joshua 7, watch for and mark any key words. Also mark the phrase *under the ban*[17] as you did last week.

As you read this chapter, carefully note the consequences of disobedience and how God has the people deal with those who are disobedient. Meditate on these things and think about how these principles apply to your own life. Remember, "these things happened to them as an example, and they were written for our instruction, upon whom the ends of the ages have come. Therefore let him who thinks he stands take heed lest he fall. No temptation has overtaken you but such as is common to man; and God is faithful, who will not allow you to be tempted beyond what you are able, but with the temptation will provide the way of escape also, that you may be able to endure it" (1 Corinthians 10:11-13).

Don't forget to mark references to geographical locations and note them on the map on page 22. Remember, if you can't locate a particular place on the map it's because the exact location is unknown.

Record the theme of Joshua 7 on the JOSHUA AT A GLANCE chart (page 48), and add any new insights to your list on Joshua.

DAY TWO

Read Joshua 8. Note how Joshua takes the city of Ai, and then note what happens after the conquest of Ai. Locate Mount Ebal and Mount Gerizim on the map (page 22).

Don't forget to add to your list on Joshua as well as putting the theme of chapter 8 on the JOSHUA AT A GLANCE chart (page 48).

DAY THREE

Read Joshua 9 and mark the key words. Be sure not to miss the word *covenant*.[18] Note what the children of Israel were obligated to do because of the gravity of making a covenant with another person. A covenant was a solemn binding agreement that, once made, was to be kept. If you have ever studied *"covenant,"** you realize that under covenant the agreeing parties were obligating themselves to defend one another. As you read, watch how the chil-

---

* If you want to do a thorough and more comprehensive study of "covenant," to see for yourself what the Scriptures say, order the inductive study course *Knowing God's Covenant*. For information on this course, call or write: Precept Ministries, P.O. Box 182218, Chattanooga, TN 37422, (615) 892-6814.

dren of Israel got into this covenant with the Gibeonites. There's a good lesson in it for each of us.

Record the theme of Joshua 9 on the JOSHUA AT A GLANCE chart (page 48) and add any insights to your list on Joshua.

DAY FOUR

Read Joshua 10 and mark any key words from your bookmark. This chapter begins Joshua's southern campaign. See the map on page 30 entitled JOSHUA'S 3-PRONGED INVASION. You might find it helpful to color each of the arrows on this map a different color. For instance, color number one red, number two blue, and number three green.

Then on the larger map, JOSHUA: OCCUPYING THE PROMISED LAND (page 22), color in blue the cities that are mentioned in chapter 10 to show that these were conquered on Joshua's second major campaign to the south.

In the margin of Joshua 10:3-5, you might want to list the five kings of the Amorites. As you make this list, remember Genesis 15:13-16 where God mentions the iniquity of the Amorites.

Note the thorough job Joshua does as he conquers every city. Record on your list any additional insights you see from marking *Joshua* in this chapter. Also put the chapter theme on the JOSHUA AT A GLANCE chart (page 48).

DAY FIVE

Read Joshua 11 and mark any key words.

Joshua's
3-Pronged
Invasion

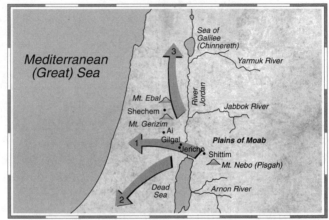

As you mark all references to locations, remember that "Chinneroth"[19] is another name for the Sea of Galilee.

At this point, note how Joshua begins his third invasion which is of the north and what provokes this invasion. Once again, look up these places on the map and color them according to your coding system. If you follow the system I gave you on Day Four, you would color them green.

Put any fresh insights on Joshua on your list in your notebook. Also, don't forget to put your theme for chapter 11 on the JOSHUA AT A GLANCE chart (page 48).

DAY SIX

Read Joshua 12 and mark any key words that you see. This brings the second segment, "The Conquest of the Land," to a close. Next week we will look at the allocation of the land. As you read, consult your map so you can keep in context.

Don't forget to record the theme of chapter 12 on the JOSHUA AT A GLANCE chart (page 48) and add your insights on Joshua to your list in your notebook.

DAY SEVEN

Store in your heart: Joshua 7:13.

Read and discuss: Genesis 2:16,17; 3:6,11; Joshua 7:10-26; 9:14.

OPTIONAL QUESTIONS FOR DISCUSSION

∾ What does God command Adam and Eve to do regarding the fruit from the tree of the knowledge of good and evil?

a. What progression of events takes place in Genesis 3:6? Watch the verbs and list them on a board.

b. What is the consequence of Eve's disobedience?

∾ What are God's commands to the children of Israel when they conquer Jericho?

a. Are these commands obeyed?

   b. What happens?

   c. When do the children of Israel realize there is sin in the camp in respect to Jericho?

   d. How is the cause of this sin discovered?

☙ When you compare Joshua 7:21 with Genesis 3:6, what do you see?

   a. What lessons can you learn for your own life in regard to this truth?

   b. What are some of the things you consider "under the ban"[20] in respect to the Christian life? Make sure your ideas can be properly supported with Scripture within its context.

   c. Is there anything in your life you have taken or you have tolerated that you feel is displeasing to God? What do you think you ought to do?

☙ What did you learn from Joshua 9:14?

   a. What do the children of Israel do in respect to the Gibeonites?

   b. Do they walk by sight or by faith? Explain your answer.

   c. How obligated are they to the Gibeonites once they make a covenant with them? Does God support them in the keeping of this covenant?

   d. Marriage is a covenant. Did you get married out of the will of God? What is your obligation? (You might want to look at Malachi 2:13-16 and mark the word *covenant*.)

☙ How did God speak to you this week? What did you learn that you can apply to your own life?

Thought for the Week

Eve knew what God said. She and Adam were forbidden to eat of one tree. Yet, when the serpent brings the tree to Eve's attention, she takes a good look at what is forbidden and finds herself desiring it. She sees, she takes, and she eats. But it doesn't stop there! She shares her sin with her husband, Adam. The consequences are awful—death for her, for Adam, and for their offspring—all of mankind.

Like Eve, Achan knew what God said: There is a ban on everything inside the walls of Jericho. Everything is to be destroyed. Nothing is to be taken. All spoils of war are forbidden this time.

Those are God's orders. Yet Achan himself said that when he saw the beautiful mantle, the silver, and the gold THEN desire crept into his heart. What he coveted, he took. And it cost not only Achan and his family their lives, but about thirty-six valiant warriors also die as a result of Achan's sin. When Joshua sends his men to take Ai, he doesn't realize there is sin in the camp. He doesn't know that someone has transgressed the covenant of the Lord—that Achan has committed a disgraceful thing in Israel. Achan disobeyed God.

What a lesson this is for us! A holy God is to be obeyed; sin must be judged. If God could not bless Israel when there was sin in the camp, He can't bless you when there is sin in your life.

Think about it, Beloved. Guard your eyes, lest you desire things God has put "under the ban" and, thus, find yourself ensnared by sin's desire. You can be sure your sins will find you out (Numbers 32:23).

Ask God to remind you that He is to be consulted in all things . . . consulted and obeyed.

What's the Cost and Reward for Saying, "I Followed the Lord My God Fully"?

DAY ONE

This week we will begin the third section of Joshua: "The Allocation of the Land" which includes chapters 13-21. Continue to mark key words as they appear. Also add to your bookmark: *inheritance*,[21] *possessed*,[22] and *promised*.[23] As you have done previously, remember to mark pronouns and synonyms that refer to the key words.

Read Joshua 13, marking your key words.

As you will observe this week, this segment of the book of Joshua deals with the portioning of the land to the various tribes of Israel. You will want to keep your map (page 22) before you so you can be in context geographically. You will also want to mark in a distinctive way every reference to the different tribes so you can easily distinguish the inheritance of each tribe.

As you do your study this week, it will be interesting to note what God gives to the twelve tribes of Israel, and what land some nations today claim as their own. You may need to refer to the map on page 22 to fully see this division.

Also add any fresh insights to your list on Joshua and write your theme for chapter 13 on the JOSHUA AT A GLANCE chart (page 48).

DAY TWO

Read Joshua 14 and 15. As you mark your key words, also watch for *Caleb*. Remember to mark pronouns that refer to him. In your notebook list everything you learn about Caleb from the text.

If you have time, read Numbers 13 and 14. If you are not familiar with the account in Numbers, it will not only give you a greater appreciation for Caleb, but will inspire you to walk in faith's obedience. In God's economy, faithfulness never goes unnoticed because God rewards the faithful.

Put the themes for Joshua 14 and 15 on your JOSHUA AT A GLANCE chart (page 48). Also add any additional insights on Joshua to the list in your notebook.

DAY THREE

Read Joshua 16 and 17 and mark key words. Note who the sons of Joseph are, how they are numbered among the tribes, and how they are given an inheritance. Watch on which side of the Jordan the inheritance falls. Once again you might want to compare this with Israel's present-day boundaries, and what the other nearby nations are claiming as theirs by referring to the map on page 37.

Don't forget to add to your list on Joshua. Record
your themes for Joshua 16 and 17 on the JOSHUA AT A
GLANCE chart (page 48).

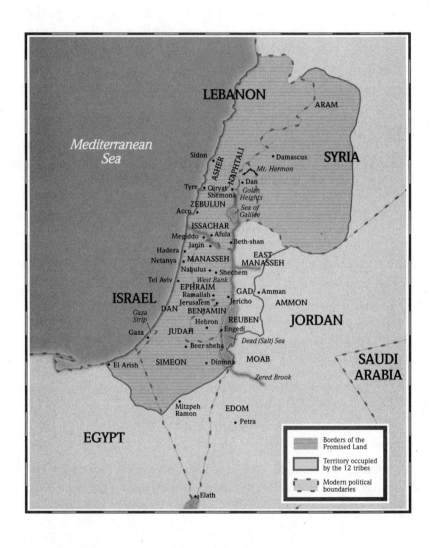

DAY FOUR

Read Joshua 18. Be sure to mark key words. Note where the tent of meeting is set up, and also note the fact that seven of the tribes still have not divided their inheritance. (I mark every reference to the tent of meeting, the tabernacle, and the temple in the same way throughout my Bible. Therefore it is easy to spot any mention of this place of worship ordained by God for the nation of Israel.) Also watch for any reference to Jerusalem, which is to become the earthly Zion, the city of God, and eventually the site of the temple.

Put the theme of chapter 18 on the JOSHUA AT A GLANCE chart (page 48) and add any additional insights to your list on Joshua.

DAY FIVE

Mark the key words as you read Joshua 19. Note what is brought to a conclusion in this chapter. Also note what Joshua inherits. Once again you might want to mark the reference to the tent of meeting. Don't forget to record your theme on the JOSHUA AT AT GLANCE chart (page 48) and add any further insights on your list on Joshua.

DAY SIX

Read Joshua 20 and 21. Mark the references to the *avenger of blood* and any other key words you see. Also note the names of the cities of refuge, why they are called cities of refuge, and how many cities there are. You might want to list these in the margin of your Bible.

When you read Joshua 21, note the three families (sons[24]) of the Levites. Also watch for any reference to the cities of refuge.

According to the Bible, to whom does the city of Hebron (the modern-day Hebron is the same) belong? Can you see how relevant this ancient book is for us today? Oh, the timelessness of the Word of God!

Pay careful attention to the last three verses of chapter 21 and think about what these verses show you about God.

Record your themes for chapters 20 and 21 on the JOSHUA AT A GLANCE chart (page 48). Also add any more insights that you gleaned from these chapters to your list on Joshua.

DAY SEVEN

Store in your heart: Joshua 21:45.

Read and discuss: Numbers 13:25–14:4,26-35; Joshua 14:6-15; 15:13-19; 21:43-45.

OPTIONAL QUESTIONS FOR DISCUSSION

∽ What did you learn about God and His promises this week?

∽ How does all that you learned compare with God's word to Joshua in Joshua 1:1-9?

∾ What did you learn from Numbers 13 and 14 in respect to:

a. believing God in difficult circumstances

b. what happens to people in times of fear or disappointment

c. standing alone

d. majority opinions

∾ What is the individual's responsibility in respect to the Word of God? Does God take note of our individual obedience or disobedience? How do you know?

∾ After studying Numbers 13 and 14 and the first 21 chapters of Joshua, what did you learn from the lives of Caleb and Joshua? How can you apply what you learned about them to your own walk with the Lord?

∾ Was God finished with Caleb or was Caleb finished with the work of God once he became 85? When do you think God is finished with a person? Why?

THOUGHT FOR THE WEEK

Believing God no matter what your eyes see, what your emotions feel, or what the "majority" tells you is not easy. You may have to stand alone. If so, that is the time to be strong and courageous, to observe to do according to all that God says in His Word, and to remember that without faith it is impossible to please God.

If, Beloved, you pass the test—if you believe and obey God, then you can rest assured that in His time and in His way you will be vindicated. Joshua and Caleb may have looked like fools the time they stood with Moses and Aaron against the angry outburst of a multitude of people who were identified as God's chosen. But, in God's eyes, it was the others who were fools because they did not believe all that God had spoken.

It took a while, but in the forty years of wandering, when all of Joshua and Caleb's contemporaries passed away in the wilderness and only Joshua and Caleb survived, it became evident that the two who chose to believe God were the only ones who were right.

O my friend, remember this: Because God is God, not one of His good promises which He has made will ever fail. What God says will come to pass. Cling to Him and His Word in faith's obedience . . . and remember: Faith is not faith until it's tested.

Pass faith's test so you can say, as Caleb said, "I followed the LORD my God fully" (Joshua 14:8).

Have You Chosen
Whom You Will Serve?

Day One

Today, we begin the final section of our study which covers chapters 22–24: "Joshua's Call to Serve the One Who Gave Them the Land." Continue to mark key words as they appear. Also add *serve, served*,[25] and *commandment(s)* to your bookmark. Don't forget to mark the synonyms and pronouns that refer to each of these words.

Read Joshua 22 and mark your key words. Compare Joshua 22:1-9 with Deuteronomy 3:18-20 and Joshua 1:10-18. Note these cross-references in the margin of your Bible.

Day Two

Read Joshua 22:10-34 and mark every occurrence of the word *altar* (along with its pronouns) and every reference to the Lord's tabernacle. When you finish, list everything you learn from marking *altar*. Note why the other tribes were concerned about the erection of this altar, and note too what they discovered about the purpose for its erection.

Record the theme for Joshua 22 on the JOSHUA AT A GLANCE chart (page 48). Also don't forget to list any fresh insights on Joshua to your notebook list.

DAY THREE

Read Joshua 23. Mark any key words you see in this chapter. As you mark any reference to their inheritance or possession, mark the phrases *this good land which the* LORD *your God has given you*[26] or *the good land which He has given you*[27] in the same way. Also in a distinctive way mark every reference to *nations*.

Add your additional insights to your list on Joshua. Also record the theme for Joshua 23 on the JOSHUA AT A GLANCE chart (page 48).

DAY FOUR

Read Joshua 23 again today. In your notebook list everything you learn from marking the occurrence of the word *nations*. Also list everything you learn about God from this chapter and add to your list on Joshua.

DAY FIVE

Review what you observed in respect to the nations yesterday in Joshua 23, then read Deuteronomy 7. Mark every reference to *nations* and list what you learn from Deuteronomy 7 regarding the nations and how it compares with Joshua 23.

Record the theme for Joshua 23 on the JOSHUA AT A GLANCE chart (page 48).

DAY SIX

Read Joshua 24 and mark the key words. Then list everything you learn from marking the word *serve*.[28] Also record any other insights about Joshua that you see from this last chapter.

Record the theme for Joshua 24 on the JOSHUA AT A GLANCE chart (page 48).

DAY SEVEN

Store in your heart: Joshua 24:14,15.
Read and discuss: Joshua 24.

OPTIONAL QUESTIONS FOR DISCUSSION

∿ What did you learn this week as you listed your insights about God from Joshua 23?

∿ What did you learn from Joshua and Deuteronomy about the nations in respect to Israel? Can you see any possible applications or lessons for your own life? Do you see anything that would help you in raising your children? Discuss your insights.

∿ When you read what the Lord says to the people through Joshua in this final chapter of the book, what do you see God doing? What is the purpose of the *therefore* in Joshua 24:14? (Since the NIV omits "therefore," here is the NASB version for your consideration: "Now, therefore, fear the LORD and serve Him in sincerity and truth; and put away the gods which your fathers served beyond the River and in Egypt, and serve the LORD.")

∾ What did you learn this week about serving the Lord? Discuss what you learned from Joshua 24 about serving the Lord and then ask the following questions:

a. What options do the children of Israel have?

b. Could anyone make their decision for them when it came to serving the Lord?

c. Who is responsible for your decision?

d. Will you be able to excuse yourself (for any reason), if you choose not to serve the Lord?

∾ If there is time, review what you recorded on the JOSHUA AT A GLANCE chart. If you are in a class setting, you might want to have the class share the most significant truth they gained in their study of this book.

THOUGHT FOR THE WEEK

Joshua, Caleb, Rahab, Achan, and the heads of the 12 tribes were all faced with decisions—decisions as to whom they were going to believe and, thus, serve. With each decision there was a course of action that followed and there was a consequence for that action. I wonder what would happen if we, as children of God, would stop and prayerfully contemplate the direction in which we are about to move, what God says about it, and what the consequences of our decision will be? Think about it, my friend. It is more than worth the time. Such action could change the course of a life . . . and even the course of a people or a nation.

What would have happened to the children of Israel had Joshua not chosen to be strong and courageous and observe to do all that God had commanded him?

What will happen to you, to your loved ones, to your people, to your nation if you choose to serve the LORD God, love the Lord your God, and walk in all His ways? What will happen if you choose not to keep His commandments, to hold fast to Him, and to serve Him with all your heart and with all your soul? Don't take a chance. Be strong and courageous! Try it and find out.

Theme of Joshua:

	SEGMENT DIVISIONS		CHAPTER THEMES
Author:			
Historical Setting:			1
			2
Purpose:			3
			4
Key Words:			5
			6
			7
			8
			9
			10
			11
			12
			13
			14
			15
			16
			17
			18
			19
			20
			21
			22
			23
			24

JUDGES

The Consequence of Partial Obedience

Special note: As you study the book of Judges, the key words you should mark will be given to you as you move through the book. Key words in this book are so specific to chapters and/or sections that a bookmark will not be helpful. Also, there is a map on page 68 to help you stay in context.

DAY ONE

Because the book of Judges is not laid out chronologically, you will find it helpful to begin your study by familiarizing yourself with the following passages. First, read Judges 1 and 2. Then read Judges 17:6; 18:1; 19:1; and 21:25 and watch for and mark in a distinctive way the key words in the verses. (At this point, see if you can find these on your own. If it isn't clear to you how to find key words, reread the second section of "How to Get Started.") This exercise will give you the setting of Judges.

DAY TWO

Read Judges 1 again. Note the timing of the book in relationship to Joshua. Watch for and mark any statement indicating that any of the tribes *did not drive out* or *did not take possession of*[1] the various people inhabiting the land. You might also want to mark every reference to the various tribes of Israel. A chart showing the camp arrangement of these tribes is found below.

Camp Arrangement of Israel's Tribes

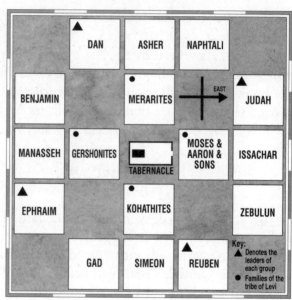

DAY THREE

The following verses are excellent cross-references for Judges 1 and for the repeated key phrases you marked yesterday. Look up these references and compare each one with Judges 1: Exodus 23:20-33; Deuteronomy 7:1-11,16; Joshua 23:5-13.

As you see the correlation between the verses in Judges and those in Exodus, Joshua, and Deuteronomy, you may want to note these verses as cross-references in the margin of your Bible. Cross-referencing helps when you may not remember the location of a passage that sheds light on or correlates with the one you are studying. Cross-referencing is also very helpful when you do not have your study notes because your notes are right in your Bible! So now write any cross-references in the margin of your Bible close to the appropriate text in Judges 1. Also write the theme for Judges 1 on the JUDGES AT A GLANCE chart (page 100).

DAY FOUR

Read Judges 2 and mark every reference to *Joshua* in a distinctive way. Then, in your notebook, list what you learn from marking Joshua. (If you have worked through the study on Joshua and listed all you learned about him in that study, you may want to add to that list.) Also note the setting of this chapter; for example, where does this chapter open geographically and what happens there?

DAY FIVE

Read Judges 2 again. This time mark in a distinctive way each reference to the *sons of Israel*[2] along with any pronouns (such as *they, them,* or *their*) or synonyms that would refer to them, such as *Israel* or *people.* Note the progression of events in this chapter by watching what the sons of Israel do and how God responds.

DAY SIX

Read Judges 2 a third time. Mark every occurrence of the words *judge* or *judges*. Then make a list of everything you observe from this chapter about the judges. Don't forget to add the theme for Judges 2 on the JUDGES AT A GLANCE chart (page 100).

DAY SEVEN

Store in your heart: Judges 21:25.
Read and discuss: Judges 2.

OPTIONAL QUESTIONS FOR DISCUSSION

∾ What did the children of Israel fail to do and how did God respond?

∾ In respect to Joshua, what is the timing of these events?

∾ What do you learn about the sons of Israel from Judges 2? What was this "generation" like and why?

∾ Judges 2 gives you an overview of the character of the times in the days of judges. From what the text says, do you see a cycle in the people's lives? What gives you this impression? What was the cycle like and why wasn't it broken? Support your answer from the text.

∾ Is there any parallel between your life and the times of the judges (as far as you have observed in Judges 1 and 2)? What is the parallel? Does anything in these two chapters give you a clue as to why there is a parallel?

ᴄᴡ What has God taught you through this week's study? Do you see any parallels to today's society? What do you think the solution might be?

THOUGHT FOR THE WEEK

You cannot expect to do what is right in your own eyes and come out a winner. If God tells you to do something, He has a valid reason for it. To disobey Him is to reap the consequences of disobedience.

In 1 Corinthians 15:33 God warns us, "Do not be deceived: 'Bad company corrupts good morals.'" The children of Israel got into trouble because they didn't drive out their enemies completely. Instead they cohabited with them. The end result was that their enemies became snares and thorns to them.

O Beloved, you cannot compromise in any way with sin—or with sinful people! At first your tolerance might be perceived as graciousness by others, for which you may be commended. However, it won't last! If you do not obey God, you'll end up with a stronghold in your life, and unless you repent with a godly sorrow, you will find yourself in a cycle of sin.

Remember the children of Israel. They **sinned.** Consequently God **sold them into the hands of** their enemies. There they remained until, in their severe distress, they **cried out to the Lord.** Then **God raised up a deliverer—a judge!** Yet because the children of Israel never really repented, never had a change of heart, their relief was only temporary. They went back into bondage again!

There is a godly sorrow that leads to repentance and life; there is a worldly sorrow that leads only to regret and death. Which will it be for you, Beloved?

Week Two

Sold into the Hands of Your Enemies! Why?

Day One

Read Judges 2:1–3:4 and mark the words *test*[3] or *testing*.[4] When you finish, write in your notebook who is testing whom, how they are being tested, and why.

Day Two

Read Judges 2 again. This time mark the phrase *the sons of Israel did evil in the sight of the LORD*.[5] Then in another distinctive way, mark the phrases *sold them into the hands of* or *gave them into the hand(s) of*. And finally mark a third phrase in yet another separately distinctive way, *the LORD raised up judges*.[6]

Day Three

Read Judges 3. Look for any parallels to the three phrases you marked yesterday in Judges 2. Mark them in the same distinctive way you marked the phrase it parallels yesterday. (In order to mark the phrases that parallel

Judges 2, you will mark: *the sons of Israel did what was evil in the sight of the LORD*[7] or *the sons of Israel again did evil in the sight of the LORD;*[8] *the LORD raised up a deliverer;*[9] and *sold them into the hands of.*) Then look for the phrase *the sons of Israel cried to the LORD*[10] and mark it in yet another distinctive way.

DAY FOUR

Read through Judges 3:3-11. Mark the references to time in a distinctive way. Remember you may want to put a clock like this 🕐 over the time phrase and/or in the margin. On pages 96-99 you will find a chart, THE JUDGES OF ISRAEL. Record on the chart what you learn about Othniel.

DAY FIVE

Read Judges 3:12-30. Once again mark every reference to time. Then record all you learn about Ehud on THE JUDGES OF ISRAEL chart (pages 96-99).

DAY SIX

Read Judges 3 again. This time mark every reference to the LORD. (Remember to mark pronouns.) If you don't want to mark all these references, at least make a list in your notebook of all you learn about the Lord from this chapter.

Record what you learn about Shamgar on the chart,
THE JUDGES OF ISRAEL (page 96-99). Then locate the
judges mentioned in Judges 3 on the chart, THE PERI-
OD OF THE JUDGES (below). Also record your theme
for Judges 3 and 4 on the JUDGES AT A GLANCE chart
(page 100).

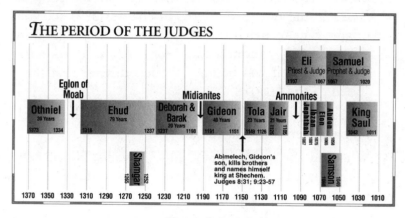

DAY SEVEN

💟 Store in your heart: Judges 3:1,2.
Read and discuss: Judges 2:20–3:31.

OPTIONAL QUESTIONS FOR DISCUSSION

∿ How does God test the sons of Israel and why? How
can you apply what you learn here to your life?
Explain your answer.

∿ Read Judges 3:3-6. Now read Deuteronomy 7:1-11 and
2 Corinthians 6:14–7:1. What parallels do you see in
these passages? What lessons do you learn for your

life? Have you seen the consequences of disobeying the principle in these verses?

∾ Discuss any parallels or relationships you observed between chapters 2 and 3 of Judges. Review the phrases you marked. Do you see any parallel between the phrase "severely distressed" in 2:15 and the sons of Israel crying out to the Lord in chapter 3? If so, you might want to mark *severely distressed*[11] in Judges 2 in the same way you marked *the sons of Israel cried to the LORD,*[12] since it was because of their distress that they "cried to the LORD."

∾ Discuss what you learned about each of the judges that are mentioned in Judges 3.

∾ What did you learn about God—His ways, His power, His ability, His heart—from this week's study?

∾ What truth struck you in the deepest way?

THOUGHT FOR THE WEEK

In Judges 1 you see a nation that is apathetic toward the commandments of the Lord. The flame of passion in the days of Joshua and the elders had hardly a spark of life left. The commandment of God was compromised. Instead of passionately obeying God and driving out the inhabitants of the land, the heathen nations were allowed by the sons of Israel to live among them. And they suffered the consequences! Their sons and daughters intermarried with people whose belief system was opposed to who God was and to the lifestyle they were to live as children of God. One of the major causes of failure in the

Christian life is tolerance of incomplete obedience to the Word of God and, thus, to the will of God!

Apathy unchecked will eventually lead to apostasy. To apostatize is to turn away from something you once believed. The sons of Israel moved from the glorious glow of victory under Joshua to the darkness of apathy's disobedience in the days of judges. Then apostasy leads to anarchy. Thus, in the days of judges, every man did what was right in his own eyes. There was no king in Israel, and they would not obey God.

Failure to worship God alone led the Israelites to following other gods . . . gods from among those of the peoples who were around them. This incurred the anger of the Lord, and rightly so. He then sold them into the hands of their enemies.

People who were meant to be free and who were to rule over their enemies were now ruled over! Yet God's character, His person, never altered. He who is rich in mercy and compassion raised up judges to deliver His people! The judge helped the situation of the people, but the people never changed their ways. For approximately 400 years, they lived in the darkness of intermittent distress and the defeat of apathy, apostasy, and anarchy.

O Beloved, never become apathetic to the Word of God or the will of God!

Put the Tent Peg in the Head of the Enemy and Sing!

D<small>AY</small> O<small>NE</small>

Read Judges 4. Mark the key phrases *the sons of Israel again did evil in the sight of the* L<small>ORD</small>,[13] *sold them into the hand of,* and *the sons of Israel cried to the* L<small>ORD</small>.[14]

D<small>AY</small> T<small>WO</small>

Today read through Judges 4 and 5. Be aware of the timing of these chapters as given in the text, and note the timing with the symbol of a clock as you did last week. Compare what you see with the chart, THE PERIOD OF THE JUDGES (page 59).

Read through Judges 4 again. As you read, keep the 5 W's and an H before you, searching out the answers to any of the questions: who, what, when, where, why, and how. (If you don't remember how to ask the 5 W's and an H, reread page 6 of "How to Get Started.")

In a distinctive color or way, mark every reference to *Deborah* (including any synonyms or pronouns). Then make a list in your notebook of what you learn about her from the text. Leave room to add more notes which you'll collect later on this week.

DAY THREE

Read through Judges 4 again marking every reference to *Barak, Sisera,* and *Jael.* (Don't forget to mark pronouns.)

DAY FOUR

List in your notebook everything you learn from Judges 4 about *Barak, Sisera,* and *Jael.* Consult the map on page 68 and note where the events of Judges 4 take place, especially where Barak and Deborah are and where each ends up.

DAY FIVE

Read Judges 5. Mark the references to *Deborah, Barak, Sisera,* and *Jael* and add your insights to the lists in your notebook. Also mark any references to time.

DAY SIX

In Judges 4 you see an account of the events in this time period of Israel's history; in Judges 5, through Deborah and Barak's account, even more details of the events of chapter 4 are filled in. Make a comparison of the two chapters.

Note what the various tribes (Ephraim, Benjamin, Zebulun, Issachar, Reuben, the half-tribe of Manasseh [see Joshua 22:9; the tribe is called Gilead here in Judges 5, giving the region occupied], Asher, Dan, and Naphtali) did or did not do.

If you have time, it would also be enlightening to mark the words *arise*[15] and *awake*[16] throughout chapters 4 and 5. Be sure to mark both words along with all their forms (i.e., *arose, rising*[17]) in the same way.

Also watch for what you can discern from chapter 5 about how the people lived during those times and exactly how God delivered them from the hand of their enemy.

Remember to record the theme for Judges 4 and 5 on the JUDGES AT A GLANCE chart (page 100).

DAY SEVEN

Store in your heart: Judges 5:2,7.
Read and discuss: Judges 4:11–5:31.

OPTIONAL QUESTIONS FOR DISCUSSION

∾ What is the progression of events in Judges 5?

∾ What did you learn about Deborah from this chapter? How does Deborah, a woman, come to be in the position she was in? (You might want to refer to what you learned about the judges in chapter 2.)

a. Discuss what the text shows you about Deborah's relationship with the Lord.

b. How does Deborah handle herself in relationship to Barak?

∾ How is Sisera conquered? What woman receives the glory, so to speak, for conquering Sisera? Recount the story from beginning to end.

Ꮿ What do you discern from Judges 4 and 5 about how the Lord routed Sisera and his iron chariots? What does this show you about the Lord?

Ꮿ What do you learn from Judges 4 and 5 about the living conditions of the people during Jabin's reign of oppression over the sons of Israel?

Ꮿ Discuss the participation—or lack of it—among the various tribes of Israel in the battle against Sisera.

Ꮿ What did you learn from Judges 4 and 5 that you can apply to your own life?

THOUGHT FOR THE WEEK

What Reuben experienced in the conflict with Sisera and the oppression of Jabin, the king of Canaan, is a good lesson for you to heed because, unfortunately, it seems to apply to so many in Christendom today. In Judges 5:15b you read that Reuben was moved to sentiment. There were "great resolves of heart," but he was not moved to sacrifice. He stayed among the sheepfolds (campfires) playing his flute for the sheep when others had gone off to war.

O Beloved, you don't want to be like Reuben! Soldiers are called to the front lines! If you don't go, if you don't do your part in facing the enemy head on, you, too, will feel the "too-late remorse" of Reuben and go through the "great searchings of heart" (5:16b).

Oh, to be able to sing Deborah and Barak's song of victory—to awake to the situation around you, and arise —arise as "a mother [or father] in Israel" (Judges 5:7). To sing because you know you did what you could when you could! To sing because when leaders lead, the people volunteer (5:2). To sing because when you step out in faith's obedience, you can know the Lord goes forth to fight and rout the enemy in His way and His time. To sing because "those who love Him [will] be like the rising of the sun in its might" (Judges 5:31).

Awake, Beloved, to your responsibility as a child of God. Do what you can, where you can, under His direction. In your own way, you will put a tent peg through the head of the enemy and then you won't be searching your heart as Reuben did!

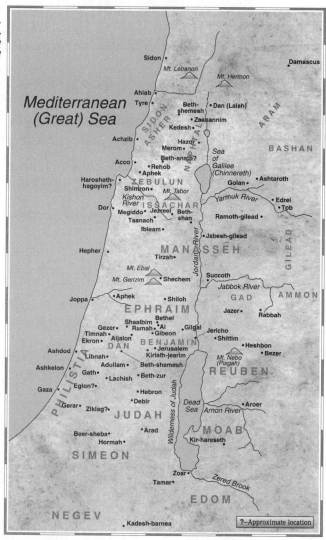

*Joshua:
Occupying
the Promised
Land*

Mediterranean
(Great) Sea

Sidon
Mt. Lebanon
Mt. Hermon
Damascus
Ahlab
Tyre
Beth-shemesh
Dan (Laish)
Zaanannim
Kedesh
Achzib
Hazor
Merom
Beth-anath?
Acco
Rehob
Aphek
Sea
of
Galilee
(Chinnereth)
Ashtaroth
Harosheth-hagoyim?
SIDON
ASHER
NAPHTALI
ZEBULUN
Shimron
Mt. Tabor
Golan
BASHAN
ARAM
Kishon
River
ISSACHAR
Yarmuk River
Edrei
Tob
Dor
Megiddo
Jezreel
Beth-shan
Ramoth-gilead
Taanach
Ibleam
Jabesh-gilead
Hepher
MANASSEH
Tirzah
Jordan River
GILEAD
Mt. Ebal
Mt. Gerizim
Shechem
Succoth
Jabbok River
Joppa
Aphek
Shiloh
GAD
AMMON
EPHRAIM
Jazer
Rabbah
Bethel
Shaalbim
Ramah
Ai
Gilgal
Gezer
Gibeon
Jericho
Timnah
Aijalon
Shittim
Ekron
BENJAMIN
Heshbon
Ashdod
DAN
Jerusalem
Bezer
Libnah
Kiriath-jearim
Mt. Nebo
(Pisgah)
Ashkelon
Adullam
Beth-shemesh
REUBEN
Gath
Lachish
Beth-zur
Eglon?
Gaza
PHILISTIA
Hebron
Gerar
Ziklag?
Debir
Dead
Sea
Arnon River
Aroer
JUDAH
MOAB
Beer-sheba
Arad
Hormah
Kir-hareseth
Wilderness of Judah
SIMEON
Zoar
Zered Brook
Tamar
EDOM
NEGEV
Kadesh-barnea
?–Approximate location

What Makes Us Valiant Warriors in God's Eyes?
(or A Trembling, Valiant Warrior?)

DAY ONE

Read through Judges 6. Again, watch for and mark the phrases that describe the repeated cycle in which the sons of Israel were caught: *the sons of Israel did what was evil in the sight of the LORD,*[18] *gave them into the hands of,*[19] and *the sons of Israel cried to the LORD.*[20] You will remember the cycle: the sons of Israel do evil, are then sold or delivered into the hands of the enemy, they cry out to the Lord, then the Lord raises up a deliverer—a judge.

Also, watch for and mark references to time and examine the text in the light of the 5 W's and an H to see what you can learn.

DAY TWO

Read Judges 6 once again. Today mark every reference to *Gideon*, and then in your notebook list all you observe from the text about him. Leave room to add to your list later. Also mark any occurrence of the word *fear*[21] or its synonym, *afraid*.

DAY THREE

Read Judges 6 once again, marking every reference to *the LORD*; *LORD, the God of Israel*;[22] *LORD your GOD*;[23] *LORD GOD*,[24] *God*. Then add what you learn from this chapter to the list you've begun on the Lord. Meditate on how He deals with the sons of Israel, and with Gideon in particular. What does Gideon discover about God? What do you discover about God?

Record the theme for Judges 6 on the JUDGES AT A GLANCE chart (page 100).

DAY FOUR

Read Judges 7. As you did in Judges 6, mark any reference to *afraid*.[25] As you read the text, keep asking the 5 W's and an H. Observe the progression of events in this chapter. When you finish, outline the chain of events covered in this chapter in your notebook.

DAY FIVE

Read through Judges 7 one more time, but instead of focusing on the events in the chapter as you did yesterday, look at God, Gideon, Gideon's men, and the Midianites. Add any new insights on Gideon to the list you began on Day 2. Add to your list on God what you learn about Him. You may also want to list what you learn about Gideon's men and the Midianites. Be sure to note how God deals with Gideon and how Gideon responds.

DAY SIX

Read Judges 8. Again mark every reference to *afraid* and any references to *Gideon*. In your notebook, list the main events of this chapter. Also add to your list what you learn about Gideon from this chapter. Be sure to note what Gideon does that becomes a snare to him and to his household and why.

Make sure you mark any time phrases. Now, fill in your information on Gideon on THE JUDGES OF ISRAEL chart (pages 96-99) and record the theme for Judges 7 and 8 on the JUDGES AT A GLANCE chart (page 100).

DAY SEVEN

Store in your heart: Judges 6:12.

Read and discuss: Judges 6:11-32; 7:1-18; 8:22-32.

OPTIONAL QUESTIONS FOR DISCUSSION

∾ What are the primary events of Gideon's life as covered in Judges 6-8?

∾ How does the end of Gideon's life compare with what you first learn about him in Judges 6?

   a. How did God deal with Gideon? Review the events of Gideon's life. What do you learn about God from His dealings with Gideon?

   b. What do you learn from the events of Gideon's

life, his responses to God, and from God's commands?

c. Are any of these insights applicable to your life and where you are today—or to how you stand in relationship to tomorrow?

∾ The book of Judges tells us that in the days of the judges every man did what was right in his own eyes. Was it right for Gideon to take the gold and make an ephod? (An ephod was used to seek guidance from God. Described in Exodus 28, it was a linen garment worn by the priest and also by David when he was king [2 Samuel 6:14]. The ephod was fastened on each shoulder by onyx clasps which had the names of six tribes engraved on one clasp and six tribes engraved on the other. The breastplate, which was fastened to the ephod, had a linen pouch *Ephod* which held the Urim and Thummin, which may have been used as sacred lots to reveal God's will [1 Samuel 28:6]. Read Exodus 28:6-30.) Discuss the validity of Gideon's actions and the results of his making this ephod.

∾ What do you learn from Gideon's actions and God's response that you can apply to your walk with the Lord?

THOUGHT FOR THE WEEK

What makes you a valiant warrior in God's eyes? Is it because you have your act together? Because you fear no foes? Because you unflinchingly move in total confidence in the Lord and His ability?

The angel of the Lord called Gideon "a valiant warrior" (Judges 6:12) when he was still a young man with no proven track record. Did God call Gideon a valiant warrior because He knew that Gideon would walk with Him, one step at a time, even though it might be in fear and trembling? Because He knew that fear or not, Gideon would recognize that "the Lord is peace"—YHWH (Jehovah) Shalom? Because He knew that Gideon would be willing to pull down his father's heathen altars, even though fear kept him from doing it in broad daylight?

Can you be a valiant warrior and still have to be reassured by "fleeces" that you are hearing correctly from command headquarters? Can you be called a valiant warrior even though you have to be reassured more than once that God will do what He said He would do—even if you have to go down to the camp to check out the situation for yourself, one last time?

Yes! You can be a valiant warrior in God's eyes if you simply keep walking by faith, no matter how shaky that faith may be at times!

Press on, valiant warrior . . . you are getting to know your God by knowing His Word. The people who know their God will be strong and do exploits (Daniel 11:32b, KJV).

Remember Gideon won by faith; Midian lost by fear!

Your Heritage Will Never Limit God

DAY ONE

Read Judges 8:29–9:22. Do you see any key phrases that have to do with Israel's cycle of sin you noted in Judges 2 and 3? Note who Abimelech is and whether or not the text indicates that he is a judge raised up by God or a self-appointed ruler.

DAY TWO

Read Judges 9. Observe the various events that occur in this chapter and who participates in these events. List your insights in your notebook.

Once again, having finished Judges 9, do you think that Abimelech would be considered one of the judges of Israel?

DAY THREE

Read Judges 10. As before, watch for and mark key phrases that show Israel's cycle during the days of the judges (*the sons of Israel again did evil in the sight of the*

LORD,[26] *sold them into the hands of, the sons of Israel cried out
to the* LORD[27]*)*. Also pay careful attention to the way God
deals with the sons of Israel when they cry out to Him, and
note how they respond.

Look at the chart, THE PERIOD OF THE JUDGES
(page 59), and note where the judges mentioned in Judges
10 fit historically. Record what you learn about the judges
mentioned in this chapter on THE JUDGES OF ISRAEL
chart (pages 96-99).

DAY FOUR

Read Judges 11. Look at the map (page 68) and note
Gilead's location. It is to the east of the Jordan River, just
north of the Jabbok River. Tob is northeast of the
Yarmuk River.

Note the events that occur in this chapter and the people involved. List them in your notebook so you can follow the chain of events in Jephthah's life.

DAY FIVE

Read Judges 12. Note whether or not Jephthah is considered a judge.

When you read of the men of Ephraim crossing over
to Zaphon (see Israelite Cities and Settlements map on
page 79) and threatening Jephthah, remember Judges 8:1-3
and the character of the times described in the verses you
looked up in Judges 17–21 in the first week of this study.

DAY SIX

Use your study time today to review what you learned in Judges 11 and 12. Record your insights on the judges mentioned in these chapters on the chart, THE JUDGES OF ISRAEL (pages 96-99). Also record the themes for Judges 9, 10, 11, and 12 on the JUDGES AT A GLANCE chart (page 100).

DAY SEVEN

Store in your heart: Judges 11:35b.
Read and discuss: Judges 11:12-40.

OPTIONAL QUESTIONS FOR DISCUSSION

∾ Besides Jephthah, what judges were covered in this week's lesson?

a. What did you learn about each of the judges? (Discuss Jephthah later.)

b. Was Abimelech a judge? What scriptures caused you to take this view?

c. What did you learn from Abimelech's life and the way the Lord dealt with him?

∾ What did you learn about Jephthah's time as a judge? How do you know he was considered a judge?

a. Discuss Jephthah's background and how God uses him despite the fact that his mother was a harlot.

b. How seriously did Jephthah take the Word of God and his commitment to God?

c. What do you see in his daughter's response to his vow? What does this response tell you about his daughter? about Jephthah? and about the seriousness of a vow?

Read Leviticus 19:12; Deuteronomy 23:21-23. (If you have time, also read Numbers 30.) Discuss these in the light of Jephthah's vow. Then, if there is time, discuss what Matthew 5:33-37 says regarding vows.

In all that you have studied this week, has the Lord spoken to you personally in a special way? Share this with the group.

THOUGHT FOR THE WEEK

A person's heritage never limits God. God not only saved the spies through Rahab the harlot in Joshua's day, but He included Rahab in the human bloodline of His Son, the Lord Jesus Christ.

God, in His time and in His way, raised up Jephthah as a judge even though he was rejected and cast out by his family because his mother was a harlot. And Jephthah proved himself a man who was serious about his commitments to his God.

How serious have you been, Beloved, about your commitment to your God and His Son, the Lord Jesus Christ? Are there vows that you have made to the Lord that you have not fulfilled? Do you call Him "Lord, Lord" and do what He would have you do, or is He "Lord" in name only?

We live in a time and society when, even among many
in the churches, people do what is right in their own eyes
because Jesus doesn't reign in them. God's eyes run to and
fro throughout the whole earth looking for men and
women whose hearts are fully His so that He might show
Himself strong on their behalf (2 Chronicles 16:9a). What
would God's eyes see in your heart?

God wants to raise up men and women He can trust
and use in these last days. Where you came from doesn't
matter! What matters is how serious you are about God's
Word and your commitment to your God.

Be His man, His woman for this hour.

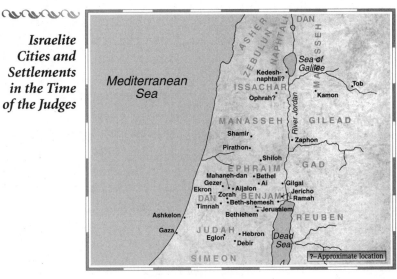

Israelite Cities and Settlements in the Time of the Judges

The Downfall and Redemption of a Macho Man

DAY ONE

This entire week will be devoted to the study of one judge, Samson, the hero of so many children's stories. After this week you will have the full story of this biblical person. As you study each chapter, take careful notes in your notebook. You may want to consolidate your notes on Samson under the major events of his life, birth, etc. This study will be most worthwhile because there is much to learn from his life!

Read Judges 13. Note the circumstances surrounding Samson's birth, who his parents are, what kind of parents they seem to be, what their concerns are, etc.

Also see if you can locate the places mentioned in these chapters on the map on page 83.

DAY TWO

Read Judges 13 again today. As you have done previously, mark any phrases that refer to Israel's cycle of doing evil, coming under their enemies, etc. *(the sons of*

Israel again did evil in the sight of the LORD,[28] *gave them into the hands of*[29]*).* Also, in a distinctive way, mark the reference to *the Spirit of the LORD,* thinking about what you learn. Mark every reference to the *Philistines.* Often today, the land of Israel is referred to as Palestine, which is incorrect. This is a name that is not biblical and should refer only to Philistia, the land of the Philistines. (See the map on page 83.)

Also mark the word *Nazirite.*[30] Note what you learn from the context of Judges 13 about a Nazirite.

DAY THREE

The vow of a Nazirite is described in Numbers 6; study it today to see what you learn about this vow. Especially note what you learn about the hair of the one taking the vow. By the way, do not confuse a Nazirite with a Nazarene, who was a person from the town of Nazareth. (Remember, Jesus was a Nazarene.) Being a Nazarene had nothing to do with long hair, drinking strong drink, or taking a vow.

DAY FOUR

Read Judges 14. Locate Timnah on the map on page 83. Mark every reference to *the Spirit of the LORD* and the *Philistines.* Note what you learn in this chapter from this event in Samson's life.

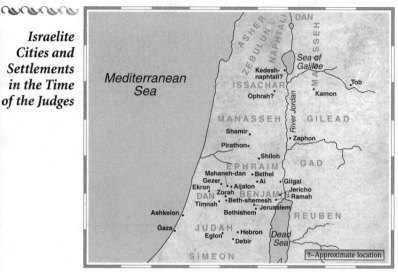

Israelite
Cities and
Settlements
in the Time
of the Judges

DAY FIVE

Read Judges 15. Continue to mark any key words you have been marking this week which appear in this chapter. Also mark any references to time. Record your insights on Samson's life from chapter 15 in your notebook.

DAY SIX

Read Judges 16. Mark the key words used in this chapter that you've been marking this week. Then carefully observe what you learn from marking them.

Also, remember what you learned about the vow of a Nazirite. Remember, too, that Samson was to be a Nazirite from his mother's womb.

Record your insights on the life of Samson in your notebook. Then add your insights to the chart, THE JUDGES OF ISRAEL (pages 96-99). Also record the theme for Judges 13, 14, 15, and 16 on the JUDGES AT A GLANCE chart (page 100).

DAY SEVEN

[♥] Store in your heart: Judges 16:28 or 16:30b.
Read and discuss: Judges 16; Hebrews 11:32-34.

OPTIONAL QUESTIONS FOR DISCUSSION

∾ What are the main events of Samson's life as recorded in the book of Judges? Review them.

∾ What did you learn about the vow of a Nazirite? How long was Samson to keep this vow? Did he?

∾ Where did Samson get his strength? What was the connection between your answer to this question and the fact that Samson lost his strength?

∾ What do you see as Samson's strengths and weaknesses?

∾ What kind of women did Samson love? What was the result of these relationships?

∾ In four chapters you went from Samson's birth to his death. What kind of a hero do you think this man is?

ᘔ When was he the most effective? Can you see any spiritual application for your own life?

ᘔ How does all that you saw this week compare with your previous impression of Samson?

ᘔ What lessons did you learn from your study of Samson's life that you can apply to your own?

THOUGHT FOR THE WEEK

Samson's eyes got him into trouble! He saw a woman in Timnah, a harlot in Gaza, and finally fell in love with a woman in the valley of Sorek—Delilah was her name!

It was the unchecked weakness of his flesh that brought Samson to impotence as a man of God. The man who knew the power of the Spirit of God upon him found himself blind, bound, and grinding at a mill. This man, who was to conquer the enemies of his people, had been conquered by his love for a woman—a love that caused him to violate his vow to God. And, thus, the Spirit of the Lord departed from him.

Was it worth it? The eyes that provoked his lust were gouged out. He who had bound others now wore chains. The man who walked away from a town carrying the city gate on his shoulders was now a grinder in prison. He who had killed a lion with his bare hands was now a source of amusement—entertainment for the ones he was supposed to have conquered. He was their blind, bound, impotent clown until he was willing to die. And in his death, he again experienced the power of the Lord. In his death he accomplished more than in his life!

And it will be the same way with you, Beloved, if you will die. What are the passions crying within your soul for fulfillment? Who is it that you think you cannot live without? Don't be a fool—don't be a Samson. Nothing . . . no one is worth losing the power of the Spirit of the Lord.

Die—reckon yourself dead—count all things as loss for the excellency of the knowledge of your Lord. Except a grain of wheat falls into the ground and dies, it abides alone . . . but if it dies it will bear much fruit. Put your passion to death, before it blinds you, binds you, and you find yourself grinding at the mill of your enemies.

Samson was more effective in the death that he consecrated than in the life he squandered! Jesus said, "If any man will come after me, let him deny himself, and take up his cross [die], and follow me" (Matthew 17:24 KJV).

Sold! For Silver, a Suit
of Clothes, and Sustenance!

DAY ONE

Read Judges 17. Note the key phrase in verse 6 and its context by asking the 5 W's and an H.

DAY TWO

Read Judges 17 again today, but this time, in a distinctive way, mark every reference to the *Levite*. Then in your notebook record all you learn about this Levite.

DAY THREE

Today you will gain further insight into a Levite and his calling and duties in respect to serving God by reading Leviticus 21:1,6-8,13-15. (Aaron was of the tribe of Levi.)

As you study today and tomorrow, mark every reference to *Aaron*, *Levi*, and *priests* in the same way you marked *Levite* in Judges 17. (Levi appears in tomorrow's reading.) All of these references are to the tribe of Levi

---

which was responsible for the worship and the tabernacle. As a matter of fact, if you completed the study on Joshua, you saw that the Levites were not given an inheritance in the land; they were to live in appointed cities, for the Lord was their inheritance.

Add your insights on the Levites to your list in your notebook.

DAY FOUR

We want to continue to look at some cross-references on the Levites so you can have a better understanding of just how bad things were in the days of the judges.

Read Numbers 25:1-13; Deuteronomy 33:8-11; Malachi 2:1-8. Continue to add insights to your list.

You might also want to put the cross-references on the Levites somewhere in the margin of Judges 17–19.

DAY FIVE

Read Judges 18. Carefully observe the main characters and events of this chapter. Mark every reference to the *priest (Levite)*, *Micah*, and the *Danites*,[31] who are sons of Dan. Then note what each does in this chapter. Add to your list.

DAY SIX

Read Judges 17 and 18 again. This time as you read, mark every reference to a *graven image*[32] *(idols,*[33] *gods).*

Then list everything you learn from this chapter about the graven image and household idols (teraphim). Also mark the reference to the *house of God* and note where the house of God was located at this time.

Don't forget to record the theme for Judges 17 and 18 on the JUDGES AT A GLANCE chart (page 100).

DAY SEVEN

Store in your heart: Judges 17:6.

Read and discuss: Judges 17:1-6,9-10; 18:27-31; Exodus 20:1-6.

OPTIONAL QUESTIONS FOR DISCUSSION

∾ Did you notice any difference in Judges 17 and 18 in comparison to the first sixteen chapters of Judges you just finished studying? What was the difference?

∾ What are Judges 17 and 18 about? Who are the main characters?

  a. What do you learn about the character of the times of the judges from reading about Micah and his mother?

  b. How far off (or biblically twisted) was Micah's thinking and his concept of God? How do you know?

  c. What do you learn about the men from the tribe of Dan in these chapters? What does this tell you about the thinking and values of the people in the days of the judges?

ॐ How does the way the Levite conducted himself (as mentioned in Judges 17 and 18) compare with God's instructions regarding the priests—those from the house of Levi?

   a. Discuss all you learned from studying the passages on the priests, the Levites.

   b. Could the Levite be bought? For what price?

ॐ What does Exodus 20:1-6 teach about idols or graven images? How does what was going on in Judges 17 and 18 compare with what you read in Exodus 20? What insights do you gain regarding the days of the judges?

ॐ Do you see any parallels between our world today and the book of Judges? Discuss these and what you see as the reason for them.

THOUGHT FOR THE WEEK

In several places in the Word, God says that we are called to be a kingdom of priests unto God, that we are to offer up spiritual sacrifices, and that we are to have nothing to do with idols.

How, beloved child of God, are you living? Are you walking in a manner worthy of your high calling in Christ, or are you doing what is right in your own eyes?

The Levite sold himself and his priesthood for a little silver, a suit of clothes, and his sustenance. O child of God, don't be caught in a snare; it cheapens and prostitutes your calling!

The Total Defeat of Doing What's Right in Your Eyes

D<small>AY</small> O<small>NE</small>

Read Judges 19 and get the setting of the events in this chapter. Its story is quite shocking.

D<small>AY</small> T<small>WO</small>

Read through Judges 19 again. Mark any reference to the *Levite* as you did last week. Note the main characters in this chapter, who they are, what they are like, and how they interact with one another. Watch also the names of the tribes that are mentioned in this chapter.

D<small>AY</small> T<small>HREE</small>

Review what you learned about the Levites last week from your list in your notebook. How do the Scriptures you studied last week on the Levites compare with what this Levite has done in respect to having a concubine and what the concubine did?

Read Judges 19:22-30. Mark the word *wickedly* along with any synonyms or pronouns that would refer to it.

Then read Genesis 19:1-29. Record what these passages
teach about homosexuality. Also in Judges 19 note the
tribe that the homosexuals were from and mark it in a distinctive way.

DAY FOUR

Read Judges 19:29–20:14. Mark every reference to the
Levite, and to the *tribe of Benjamin* or *the sons of
Benjamin*.[34] Mark the references to *Benjamin* (and *Gibeah*
since Gibeah belonged to Benjamin), along with every reference to *wickedness*.[35] Also mark *lewd*[36] and *disgraceful
act(s)*[37] in the same way you mark *wickedness* since they
refer to wicked actions.

After you read, think about what is going on and why.

DAY FIVE

Read Judges 20:12-48. Mark every reference to the
tribe of Benjamin or *sons of Benjamin*[38] or *Gibeah* as you
did yesterday. Also mark every occurrence of the phrase
the *sons of Israel*[39] and *men of Israel*.

Three battles are described in this chapter. Carefully
distinguish one from another. Note what the sons of
Israel do before each battle, and what the outcome of each
battle is.

When you finish observing this chapter, you will find
it enlightening to add up the total number of casualties
and note why they died.

DAY SIX

Read Judges 21. Once again mark the references to the *sons of Israel*,[40] *men of Israel,* and to *sons of Benjamin.*[41]

As you read this chapter, note what the problem or dilemma is and how they solve it. And then observe the conclusion of it all!

Record the theme for Judges 19, 20, and 21 on the JUDGES AT A GLANCE chart (page 100).

DAY SEVEN

Store in your heart: Judges 19:30.
Read and discuss: Judges 19:22–20:13.

OPTIONAL QUESTIONS FOR DISCUSSION

ᵔ By way of review, what is the content of the final five chapters of Judges?

    a. Do these chapters record anything concerning the judges of Israel?

    b. Why do you think God included these accounts in chapters 17–21 in the book of Judges which covers about 350 years of Israel's history?

ᵔ How did studying the last three chapters of Judges affect you?

    a. How applicable do you believe these chapters are to today and why?

b. In what way do you feel these chapters apply to today? What parallels do you see?

c. What can you learn from these chapters?

⌘ A Levite is involved in the events of each of these final five chapters. Does this tell you anything about the spiritual tenor of the times? Do you see any parallels to today?

⌘ How do you see the people of the nation of Israel dealing with their problems? Is it in a biblical way? Explain your answer. What does this tell you about the times?

⌘ How costly were their actions in dealing with their problems?

⌘ What does the way the tribe of Benjamin dealt with the issue of judging the homosexual men's behavior tell you about the times?

a. What does the Word of God say about homosexuality? Have the class share pertinent Scriptures. If they do not know any, look up the following and discuss them: Leviticus 18:22; 20:13 (20:10-21); Romans 1:26-27 (1:18-32); 1 Corinthians 6:9-11.

b. Do you see any parallel between protecting homosexuality and all who have contracted and died from AIDS as a result of this sin, when you think of all the deaths that occurred in Judges 20 because of their unwillingness to judge sin? Does sin pollute a land as God says?

⌘ What is the most significant truth or principle that you have learned from the book of Judges? How are you going to live in the light of it?

THOUGHT FOR THE WEEK

Apathy leads to apostasy and apostasy can only lead to anarchy. Anarchy comes when every man does what is right in his own eyes because he has no king except himself!

How similar our days are to the days of judges! Churches are filled with people who are caught in idolatry for, according to Colossians 3:5, greed is idolatry. Immorality is pervasive. Homosexuality is tolerated and rationalized. Many churches are filled with internal strife as brother wars against brother. And then, when resolution is needed, instead of fasting, weeping, and repenting we try to solve our problems in our own way even as they did in Judges 21.

We forget that because we were born in sin, because we live in a body of flesh, we need not only a Savior but also a Lord. We need Someone to rule over us; Someone to direct our paths; Someone who has infinite wisdom, patience, and love. If we do not allow our Lord to rule over us, if we are not strong and courageous to do according to all He has commanded us, then Beloved, we will be conquered by the pressures of the world around us, and the futility of our own reasoning.

Bow before King Jesus!

THE JUDGES OF ISRAEL

Judge / Chapter & Verse   Insights

_____

_____

_____

_____

_____

_____

_____

_____

_____

_____

_____

_____

_____

_____

_____

_____

_____

_____

_____

_____

_____

_____

_____

_____

_____

_____

_____

_____

_____

THE JUDGES OF ISRAEL

Judge / Chapter & Verse   Insights

_____

_____

_____

_____

_____

_____

_____

_____

_____

_____

_____

_____

_____

_____

_____

_____

_____

_____

_____

_____

_____

_____

_____

_____

_____

_____

_____

_____

THE JUDGES OF ISRAEL

Judge / Chapter & Verse   Insights

_____

_____

_____

_____

_____

_____

_____

_____

_____

_____

_____

_____

_____

_____

_____

_____

_____

_____

_____

_____

_____

_____

_____

_____

_____

THE JUDGES OF ISRAEL

Judge / Chapter & Verse   Insights

_____

_____
_____
_____
_____
_____
_____
_____
_____
_____
_____
_____
_____
_____
_____
_____
_____
_____
_____
_____
_____
_____
_____
_____
_____
_____
_____
_____
_____
_____
_____
_____
_____

Theme of Judges:

SEGMENT
DIVISIONS

			CHAPTER THEMES	Author:
		1		Date:
		2		Purpose:
		3		
		4		Key Words:
		5		sons of Israel did evil in the sight of the LORD
		6		
		7		
		8		sold (served) into the hands of
		9		
		10		sons of Israel cried out to the LORD
		11		
		12		the LORD raised up a deliverer (or judge)
		13		judge(s)
		14		
		15		
		16		
		17		
		18		
		19		
		20		
		21		

RUTH

When You Choose the Refuge of His Wings . . .

DAY ONE

Read the first chapter of Ruth to get the setting of this short but dynamic book. As you read, carefully observe the historical and geographical setting of the book of Ruth.

When you come to any reference to time, draw a clock like this: 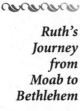 over the phrase or in the margin of your

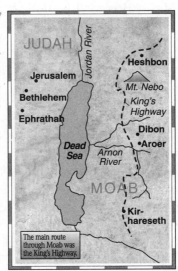

Ruth's Journey from Moab to Bethlehem

Bible next to the verse that shows you the "when" of the events of this first chapter.

Carefully observe the main characters and the main events in this chapter. Consult the map on page 103 to put yourself into context geographically.

You may have heard others quote Ruth 1:16,17. Note the context of these verses: who is saying them, to whom, when, why, and under what circumstances?

Record the main theme of chapter 1 on the RUTH AT A GLANCE chart (page 109).

DAY TWO

Read Ruth 2 and mark every reference to *Boaz*. Also mark every occurrence of *relative*,[1] *closest relatives*[2] and *kinsman*. When you finish, list in your notebook what you learn about Boaz from the text.

DAY THREE

Reread Ruth 1 and 2. List what you learn about Ruth from these two chapters. (You may want to mark every reference to her in a distinctive color or way as you read back through these two chapters.) What kind of woman do the Scriptures portray Ruth to be? Does it go unnoticed?

Record the theme of chapter 2 on the RUTH AT A GLANCE chart (page 109).

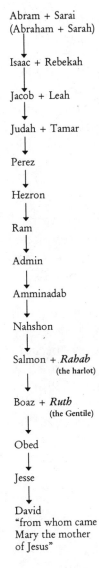

The Genealogy of Boaz

Abram + Sarai
(Abraham + Sarah)
↓
Isaac + Rebekah
↓
Jacob + Leah
↓
Judah + Tamar
↓
Perez
↓
Hezron
↓
Ram
↓
Admin
↓
Amminadab
↓
Nahshon
↓
Salmon + *Rahab*
              (the harlot)
↓
Boaz + *Ruth*
              (the Gentile)
↓
Obed
↓
Jesse
↓
David
"from whom came
Mary the mother
of Jesus"

DAY FOUR

Read Ruth 3 today. As you read, mark the following words, each in a distinctive way: *kinsman*[3] *(close relative,*[4] *relative*[5]*)* and *redeem.*[6] Note how Ruth is described in this chapter, and add your insights to the list you began yesterday.

Note the events that take place in this chapter then record the main theme of this chapter on the RUTH AT A GLANCE chart (page 109).

DAY FIVE

The fourth chapter of Ruth brings our love story to a conclusion. Read it carefully and once again mark the words you marked yesterday in their various forms, i.e., *redeem,*[7] *redemption,*[8] or *close* or *closest relative,*[9] or *redeemer.*[10] Add anything new you see about Ruth to your list.

As you read, note THE GENEALOGY OF BOAZ chart on this page. You will see that the name Admin is on the chart. Also, as you study this, note Rahab's relationship to Boaz. Look up Luke 3:32 and Matthew 1:5 for further insights. Remember what you learned about Rahab in your study of the book of Joshua. (If you haven't studied Joshua yet, you will be excited about this truth when you do!)

DAY SIX

To really appreciate what takes place in Ruth 3 and 4, you need to familiarize yourself with the laws of redemption in Leviticus 25:23-28. In the Leviticus passage, mark any reference to the two key words you have marked in Ruth: *relative*[11] *(kinsman*[12] or *nearest kinsman*[13]) and *redemption.*[14]

Now read Deuteronomy 25:5-10. Note what you learn from this passage that relates to what you have read in the book of Ruth—there is a correlation between them. You may want to note these verses which correlate to one another as cross-references in the margin of your Bible. Cross-referencing helps when you may not remember the location of a passage that sheds light on or correlates with the one you are studying. Cross-referencing is also very helpful when you do not have your study notes—because your notes are right in your Bible! So now, write the cross-references from Deuteronomy in the margin of your Bible close to the appropriate text in Ruth.

Record the main theme of chapter 4 on the RUTH AT A GLANCE chart (page 109).

DAY SEVEN

Store in your heart: Ruth 2:12.
Read and discuss: Ruth 4 and Genesis 38.

Optional Questions for Discussion

ॐ What interested you the most about the book of Ruth? Why?

ॐ At what period of time does this book take place? Discuss what you observed in chapter 1 about the historical and geographical setting.

ॐ What do you learn about the role of the "kinsman" from the book of Ruth?

ॐ What do you learn about the responsibility to childless widows in biblical times? How does Boaz compare with what you read about Judah in Genesis 38?

ॐ What did you learn about the character of Ruth from this book?

ॐ What lessons did you learn from studying the characters in this book that you can now apply to your own life as a man, a woman, a mother-in-law, a daughter-in-law, or a relative?

ॐ When you look at the women in the genealogy of our Lord Jesus Christ, and since God is sovereign, what do you learn about God as He selects those to be in His Son's earthly "genealogical tree"?

ॐ The book of Ruth occurs during the time of judges, when every man did what was right in his own eyes. How does what you learn about Ruth compare with the spirit of the children of Israel at that time? (The Spirit of the children of Israel is covered in the book of Judges; if you haven't studied Judges yet, you probably can't respond to this question.)

THOUGHT FOR THE WEEK

Nobility of character is a rare thing in our times when multitudes do what is right in their own eyes.

Ruth, who is referred to as a woman of excellence (3:11), made a choice—a choice that showed her character and respect for her position and responsibility as a wife and as a daughter-in-law. Her choice did not go unnoticed in the eyes of God or in the eyes of the community.

What Ruth lost in the death of her husband was gained in "death to self." Ruth chose the way of honor. God then honored her by putting a "Gentile" woman in the birth line of His Son. Ruth would have the honor of bringing forth Obed, and Obed would bring forth Jesse, the father of David, the king of Israel, a man after God's own heart. And as you know, it is from David that Mary, Jesus' mother, descended.

Ruth will be in the resurrection of the righteous because she chose Naomi's God as her God. The Lord rewarded her work. Her wages were full from the Lord, the God of Israel, under whose wings she sought and found the refuge she needed.

O Beloved, let's raise up another generation—a godly seed, a generation of men and women who want to live nobly, sacrificially, rather than living for self and doing what is right in their own eyes.

Let's model this lifestyle for others . . . and then call them to follow us even as we are followers of our Lord Jesus Christ. We can remind them that the same Lord will reward their work if they will but seek refuge under His wings by making choices that will please Him and reflect who He is.

Theme of Ruth:

	SEGMENT DIVISIONS	
Author:		CHAPTER THEMES
Date:		1
Purpose:		
Key Words:		
redeem (redemption)		2
relative (closest relative, kinsman)		
Naomi		
Ruth		3
Boaz		
		4

Notes

Joshua

1. NIV: also uses *country, region, territory, area, plain, border*
   KJV; NKJV: also uses *country*
2. NIV: also uses *stronger, powerful*
3. KJV; NKJV: also uses *of a good courage* or *of good courage*
4. KJV; NKJV: *commandment, word*
5. NIV: also uses *tell, word, directed, ordered, giving orders, instructed, gave the order, gave*
   KJV: also uses *commandest, charged*
   NKJV: also uses *commandment, word, charged*
6. NIV: *occupy, for your own*
   KJV: also mark *have possessed*
7. NIV: also uses *occupy, acquired*
   KJV; NKJV: also uses *drive out*
8. NIV; KJV; NKJV: also uses *Israelites*
9. NIV: also mark *did so* as it refers to *circumcised*
10. NIV: does not use *circumcising*
11. NIV; NKJV: *be afraid*
12. NIV: also uses *make war*
13. NIV: also uses *attacked, was fighting, fight*
    KJV: also uses *fight, warred*
    NKJV: also uses *fight*
14. NIV; NKJV: also uses *took, taken*
    KJV: *took, take, taken*
15. NIV: *keep away from devoted things*
    KJV: *accursed thing*
    NKJV: also uses *doomed . . . to destruction*
16. KJV: uses Rachab in this passage of Scripture.
17. NIV: *devoted*
    KJV; NKJV: *accursed*
18. NIV: also uses *treaty*
    KJV: also uses *league*
19. NIV: "Kinnereth"

20. NIV: *keep away from devoted things*
    KJV: *accursed thing*
21. NIV: also *inheritances*
    KJV; NKJV: also uses *inherit*
22. NIV: *taken over*
23. KJV; NKJV: *said*
24. NIV: *decendants* or *clans*
    KJV: *children*
25. NIV: also uses *serving, worshiped*
26. NIV: *this good land, which the LORD your God has given you* or *this good land he has given you*
    KJV: *this good land which the LORD your God hath given you*
27. NIV: *the good land he has given you*
    KJV: *the good land which he hath given unto you*
    NKJV: *the good land which He has given you*
28. NIV: also *serving*

JUDGES

1. NIV: also *unable to drive . . . from, failed to dislodge,* or *never drove them out*
2. NIV: *Israelites*
   KJV: *children of Israel*
3. KJV: *prove*
4. NIV: only uses the word *test*
5. NIV: *the Israelites did evil in the eyes of the LORD*
   KJV; NKJV: *the children of Israel did evil in the sight of the LORD*
6. NIV: also *the LORD raised up a judge*
   KJV: also *the LORD raised them up judges*
7. NIV: *the Israelites did evil in the eyes of the LORD*
   KJV; NKJV: *the children of Israel did evil in the sight of the LORD*
8. NIV: *once again the Israelites did evil in the eyes of the LORD*
   KJV: *the children of Israel did evil again in the sight of the LORD*
   NKJV: *the children of Israel again did evil in the sight of the LORD*
9. NIV: *he raised up for them a deliverer* or *he gave them a deliverer*
   KJV: *the LORD raised them up a deliverer*
10. NIV: *they cried out to the LORD* or *the Israelites cried out to the LORD*
    KJV: *the children of Israel cried unto the LORD*

11. NIV: *in great distress*
    KJV; NKJV: *greatly distressed*

12. NIV: *they cried to the* LORD or *the Israelites cried out to the* LORD
    KJV: *the children of Israel cried unto the* LORD

13. NIV: *the Israelites once again did evil in the eyes of the* LORD
    KJV; NKJV: *the children of Israel again did evil in the sight of the* LORD

14. NIV: *they cried to the* LORD
    KJV: *the children of Israel cried unto the* LORD
    NKJV: *the children of Israel cried out to the* LORD

15. NIV: also *go*
    KJV; NKJV: also *up*

16. NIV: *wake up*

17. NIV: *rises*
    KJV: *goeth forth*
    NKJV: *when it comes out*

18. NIV: *the Israelites did evil in the eyes of the* LORD
    KJV; NKJV: *the children of Israel again did evil in the sight of the* LORD

19. KJV; NKJV: *delivered them into the hand of*

20. NIV: *the Israelites cried out to the* LORD
    KJV: *the children of Israel cried unto the* LORD
    NKJV: *the children of Israel cried out to the* LORD

21. KJV; NKJV: also *feared*

22. KJV; NKJV: LORD *God of Israel*

23. KJV: also uses LORD *thy God*

24. NIV: *sovereign* LORD

25. KJV: *fearful*

26. NIV: *the Israelites did evil in the eyes of the* LORD
    KJV: *the children of Israel did evil again in the sight of the* LORD
    NKJV: *the children of Israel again did evil in the sight of the* LORD

27. NIV: *the Israelites cried out to the* LORD
    KJV: *the children of Israel cried unto the* LORD
    NKJV: *the children of Israel cried out to the* LORD

28. NIV: *the Israelites did evil in the eyes of the* LORD
    KJV: *the children of Israel did evil again in the sight of the* LORD
    NKJV: *the children of Israel did evil in the sight of the* LORD

29. NIV; KJV; NKJV: *delivered them into the hand(s) of*

30. KJV: *Nazarite*

31. KJV: also *children of Dan*

32. NIV: also *carved image*

33. KJV: *teraphim*

34. NIV: *Benjamites*
    NKJV: *children of Benjamin*
35. NIV: *awful thing, awful crime, evil*
    KJV: also *evil*
    NKJV: also *wicked deed, evil*
36. KJV; NKJV: *lewdness*
37. NIV: *vileness*
    KJV: *folly*
    NKJV: *vileness, outrage*
38. NIV: *Benjamites*
    KJV; NKJV: *children of Benjamin*
39. NIV: *Israelites*
    KJV; NKJV: *children of Israel*
40. NIV: *Israelites*
    KJV; NKJV: *children of Israel*
41. NIV: *Benjamites*
    KJV; NKJV: *children of Benjamin*

RUTH

1. NIV: also *close relative*
   KJV: *near of kin*
2. NIV: *kinsman-redeemers*
   KJV: *next kinsmen*
   KJV: *near kinsmen*
3. KJV: *kindred*
4. NIV: *kinsman-redeemer, near of kin*
   KJV; NKJV: *near kinsman*
5. KJV; NKJV: *kinsman*
6. NIV: also *do it*
   KJV: *perform . . . the part of a kinsman, do the kinsman's part, do the part of a kinsman*
   NKJV: *perform the duty of a near kinsman, do it, perform the duty*
7. NIV: also *do* or *next in line*
8. KJV; NKJV: *redeeming*
9. NIV: *kinsman-redeemer*
   KJV: *kinsman*
10. NIV: *kinsman-redeemer*
    KJV: *kinsman*
    NKJV: *near kinsman*

11. NIV: *countryman*
    KJV; NKJV: *brother*
12. NIV: *one*
13. NIV: *nearest relative*
    KJV: *kin*
    NKJV: *kinsman-redeemer*
14. NIV; KJV; NKJV: also *redeem*

Books in the
International Inductive Study Series

Also by Kay Arthur

How to Study Your Bible

Beloved

His Imprint, My Expression

My Savior, My Friend

God, Are You There?

Lord, Teach Me to Pray in 28 Days

With an Everlasting Love

Israel, My Beloved

THE INTERNATIONAL INDUCTIVE STUDY BIBLE IS

Changing the Way People Study God's Word

 *I*T IS A REVOLUTIONARY IDEA whose time has come....a study Bible that actually teaches you *how* to study the Bible. As you follow simple, easy-to-understand instructions, you will discover God's truth on your own. In *The International Inductive Study Bible*, you will find maps right in the text where you need them, timeline charts showing biblical events in historical order, wide margins in which to write your notes, the accurate and reliable New American Standard Bible text, and dozens of other helpful features. This proven study method will lead you to experience God's Word in a way so personal, so memorable, that every insight you gain will be yours for life.

HARVEST HOUSE PUBLISHERS

1075 Arrowsmith, Eugene OR 97402

At bookstores everywhere!

WHY THESE AND MANY OTHER CHRISTIAN LEADERS ARE SUPPORTING THIS REVOLUTION IN STUDY BIBLES:

BILL BRIGHT
"...one of the best tools that you could possibly use..."

R.C. SPROUL
"...this is a user-friendly approach to learning Scripture..."

JOSH McDOWELL
"...discover the truth for yourself."

RUTH BELL GRAHAM
"...I'm sold on it."

❏ **YES!** I am interested in information that will direct me to an Inductive Bible study group in my area *or* that will help me or my church become involved in inductive Bible study.

❏ I am interested in further training on how to study my Bible inductively. Please send me information on how to know God and His Word in a more personal way.

I have used this book

    ❏ in personal devotions and/or study

    ❏ in Sunday school

    ❏ in small group study

    ❏ in church

    ❏ in the community

    ❏ in connection with the radio program "Precept with Kay Arthur."

❏ I have received Jesus Christ as my Lord and Savior as a result of this study. Please send me literature that will help me become established in God's Word.

Name of this book _____

Name _____

Address _____

City/State/Zip _____

Daytime telephone (_____) _____

Precept Ministries exists for the sole purpose of establishing God's people in His Word. We desire to help you minister more effectively to others.

BUSINESS REPLY MAIL
FIRST-CLASS MAIL   PERMIT NO. 48   CHATTANOOGA TN

POSTAGE WILL BE PAID BY ADDRESSEE

PRECEPT MINISTRIES
P O BOX 182218
CHATTANOOGA TN 37422-9901

NO POSTAGE
NECESSARY
IF MAILED
IN THE
UNITED STATES